RESEARCH HIGHLIGHTS IN SOCIAL WORK 30

Children and Young People in Conflict with the Law

Research Highlights in Social Work Series

Social Work with Adult Offenders
Edited by Joyce Lishman
ISBN 0 9505999 4 8 hb
Research Highlights in Social Work 5

Working With Children
Edited by Joyce Lishman
ISBN 1 85302 007 9 hb
Research Highlights in Social Work 6

Collaboration and Conflict: Working with Others
Edited by Joyce Lishman
ISBN 0 9505999 6 4 hb
Research Highlights in Social Work 7

Approaches to Addiction
Edited by Joyce Lishman and Gordon Horobin
ISBN 1 85091 000 6 hb
ISBN 1 85091 001 4 pb
Research Highlights in Social Work 10

Responding to Mental Illness
Edited by Gordon Horobin
ISBN 1 85091 005 7 hb
Research Highlights in Social Work 11

The Family: Context or Client?
Edited by Gordon Horobin
ISBN 1 85091 026 X hb
Research Highlights in Social Work 12

Sex, Gender and Care Work
Edited by Gordon Horobin
ISBN 1 85302 001 X hb
Research Highlights in Social Work 15

Living with Mental Handicap: Transitions in the Lives of People with Mental Handicap
Edited by Gordon Horobin and David May
ISBN 1 85302 004 4 hb
Research Highlights in Social Work 16

Child Care: Monitoring Practice
Edited by Isobel Freeman and Stuart Montgomery
ISBN 1 85392 005 2 hb
Research Highlights in Social Work 17

Social Work and Health Care
Edited by Rex Taylor and Jill Ford
ISBN 1 85302 016 8 hb
Research Highlights in Social Work 19

Social Work: Disabled People and Disabling Environments
Edited by Michael Oliver
ISBN 1 85302 042 7 hb
ISBN 1 85302 178 X pb
Research Highlights in Social Work 21

Poverty, Deprivation and Social Work
Edited by Ralph Davidson and Angus Erskine
ISBN 1 85302 043 5 hb
Research Highlights in Social Work 22

Social Work and the European Community: The Social Policy and Practice Contexts
Edited by Malcolm Hill
ISBN 1 85302 091 5 hb
Research Highlights in Social Work 23

Child Abuse and Child Abusers: Protection and Prevention
Edited by Lorraine Waterhouse
ISBN 1 85302 408 2 pb
Research Highlights in Social Work 24

Developments in Short-Term Care: Breaks and Opportunities
Edited by Kirsten Stalker
ISBN 1 85302 134 2 pb
Research Highlights in Social Work 25

Working with Offenders
Edited by Gill McIvor
ISBN 1 85302 249 7 pb
Research Highlights in Social Work 26

Planning and Costing Community Care
Edited by Chris Clark and Irvine Lapsley
ISBN 1 85302 267 5 pb
Research Highlights in Social Work 27

Social Work and People with Mental Health Problems
Edited by Marion Ulas and Anne Connor
ISBN 1 85302 302 7 pb
Research Highlights in Social Work 28

Developing Services for Older People and their Families
Edited by Rosemary Bland
ISBN 1 85302 290 X pb
Research Highlights in Social Work 29

RESEARCH HIGHLIGHTS IN SOCIAL WORK 30

Children and Young People in Conflict with the Law

Edited by Stewart Asquith

Jessica Kingsley Publishers
London and Bristol, Pennsylvania

Robert Gordon University
School of Applied Social Studies
Kepplestone Annexe, Queen's Road
Aberdeen AB9 2PG

First published in the United Kingdom in 1996 by
Jessica Kingsley Publishers Ltd
116 Pentonville Road
London N1 9JB, England
and
1900 Frost Road, Suite 101
Bristol, PA 19007, U S A

Library of Congress Cataloging in Publication Data
A CIP catalogue record for this book is available from the Library of Congress

British Library Cataloguing in Publication Data
A CIP catalogue record for this book is available from the British Library

ISBN 1-85302-291-8

Printed and Bound in Great Britain by
Cromwell Press, Melksham, Wiltshire

Contents

List of Tables

Acknowledgements

This book would not have been possible without the encouragement, persuasion and sheer perseverance of a number of people. In particular, Joyce Lishman, editor of the Research Highlights Series, is due considerable thanks for making sure that we stuck to our task and did not exceed our deadline by too much. I'm also aware that the contributors produced their chapters in the context of the many competing demands on their time, and they should know that their efforts have been greatly appreciated. The Computing Service at the University of Glasgow also provided invaluable help in translating those contributions on disc which appeared in a variety of formats. The Centre for the Study of the Child and Society has been fortunate to have the services of experienced and committed secretarial staff and, as in so many instances in the work of the Centre, this book would not have seen the light of day without the substantial contribution of Laura Lochead and Elaine Hodge. None of those mentioned, though, bear any responsibility either for any editorial mistakes or editorial judgements made about the content of the book – these are entirely my responsibility.

Stewart Asquith

Introduction

Stewart Asquith

As an introduction to the chapters included in this volume, a number of general comments will be made about the relationship between explanations of offending by children and young people, and the implications these have for the development of relevant and effective crime prevention strategies.

Throughout Europe systems of juvenile justice and delinquency control are presently being reviewed, with current preoccupations focusing on the relationship between a 'welfare' and a more traditional 'justice and punishment' approach to dealing with children and young people who offend (Asquith 1995). Indeed this has been a recurring theme in the history of juvenile justice this century, and in many respects the ongoing examination of the philosophies, and practices and polices based on them, reflects the changing nature of offending; how offending is explained and the nature of the threat posed to social life through offending behaviour by children and young people.

In addition, current reconsideration of the approaches and measures adopted to deal with those children and young people who offend is also influenced by the increasing obligation and commitment to recognising the rights of those young people caught up in formal juvenile and criminal justice systems. Concern with the rights of children and young people who offend was acknowledged as of central significance for any just system of delinquency crime in reaction to such cases as in re Gault in the 1960s and has more recently been the subject of international attention through the Riyadh guidelines, the Beijing Rules and of course the United Nations Convention on the Rights of the Child (Asquith 1995; Cappelaere 1995) adopted by the United

Nations General Assembly in 1989 and ratified by the United Kingdom government in 1991.[1]

There have of course recently been a number of changes in the ways in which those children and young people who offend are dealt with in Scotland and in England and Wales, and the Scottish and English and Welsh systems are examined in some detail later in this book. However, many of the trends in the nature and profile of offending by the young are manifested more broadly in the international arena with reviews of juvenile justice systems and measures for dealing with juvenile delinquency being undertaken in most European countries. For these reasons, it is important to consider developments in the United Kingdom in a broader context and for that reason a number of the chapters in this book refer to what is happening in a number of European countries, particularly in the changing social, economic and political climate of Central and Eastern Europe. Similarly, the drive to review systems of juvenile justice can be better appreciated by locating them in the context of more general trends in offending by children and young people.

Trends in juvenile delinquency

The general increase in crime in Western Europe since the Second World War, and in particular the increase in crime by children and young people, is a well-documented phenomenon. What is also known is that there has been a reduction in the crime figures from the mid-1980s onwards and this is also reflected in an accompanying decrease in the number of crimes committed by juveniles (Asquith 1992a).

There are, however, a number of difficulties which have to be addressed in seeking to interpret such broad trends, the significance of which is that they are directly related to very basic questions about just what is taken to be juvenile delinquency and what is the best and most appropriate means of dealing with it. As stated elsewhere (Asquith 1995), measures for dealing with offending behaviour do have to bear some relationship to how delinquency is conceived of, otherwise preventive and control programmes will be ineffective.

---

1 The importance of the UN Convention in its implication for all those social institutions which relate to children is illustrated by the fact that almost 200 countries around the world have now ratified the Convention.

In the first instance, it is by no means clear what is meant by 'juvenile' and what we mean by 'delinquency'. Throughout Western Europe, the age of criminal responsibility and penal majority differs considerably. For example, in Scotland though there is a unique system of juvenile justice based on welfare principles, the age of criminal responsibility remains at 8, though few children are prosecuted until they reach 13. In England and Wales, the age of criminal responsibility rests at 10 with distinctions made between children who are 10 but not yet 14, and young persons who are between 14 and 17. In Germany, the distinctions are drawn between children under 14, adolescents between 14 and 18, and young adults between 18 and 21. Dunkel provides a useful overview of the variability in justice systems throughout Europe (Dunkel 1991). The main point to be made here is that the development of measures to deal with juvenile delinquency in different countries reflects very different notions of just to whom the concept 'juvenile' applies.

Moreover, the issue of age has also to be seen in relation to the very different justice systems in which children and juveniles are dealt with. Scotland has no juvenile court and the majority of children who commit offences are dealt with by the Children's Hearings system. The Children's Hearings, which have no punitive sanctions available, deal with the majority of children who are deemed to be in need of compulsory measures of care, whether they have committed an offence or not. In England, many more children who commit offences are cautioned by the police with the result that a smaller proportion of children actually go to court. Again, the main point to make here is that the difficulty of international comparisons is compounded by the different conceptions held of children who commit offences and how to deal with them. The very different notions of 'children' and 'juvenile' are reflected in the response of justice systems and also in the way they relate to other organisations and institutions such as social work and child care services. They are also related to very different cultural notions and expectations of childhood, the family and the role of the state. The significance of this line of argument is that the reduction in juvenile crime which we will identify more clearly later has to be seen in relation to changes in the way children who commit offences are being dealt with. Barclay and Turner (1991, p.81) makes the point neatly by asserting that 'these reflect differences in the methods used to handle juvenile offending rather than large scale differences in offending behaviour'.

As regards the notion of 'delinquency' there are of course further problems. In particular, most of our European information on delinquency or at least on crime has been until recently based on official statistics of crimes and offences reported to and recorded by the police. At least two difficulties can be presented here.

One is that delinquency is taken to mean offences committed by children and young people above a certain age and who are subject to lawful intervention for offence behaviour. The difficulty here, if we are serious about our wish to reduce juvenile delinquency, is that many children have started on a delinquent career well before they reach the legal age at which they can be dealt with formally. This has important implications for the development of preventive measures, programmes and policies; and, in particular, identifies the early years of children's lives as an appropriate site for the location of preventive strategies.

The second and most problematic issue is that the official police and other statistics do of course only tell us about delinquency reported and recorded by the police. Again, given what we have said about the very different age classifications, the different nature of justice systems and the different approaches to dealing with delinquency, some scepticism has to be expressed about the reliability of the information on which we base our understanding of and our measures to deal with delinquency (see Anderson 1994).

What is clear from research done throughout Europe in the form of victimisation and self report studies is that there is a greater level of offending behaviour in which children and young people are involved than the official statistics suggest. The value of such studies is that they expand our knowledge of the numbers of children involved in delinquency who do not appear in the statistics. They also at the same time provide much-needed information about the changing pattern of delinquency careers and the relationship to later adult criminal behaviour.

Notwithstanding such difficulties – which are not by any means simply semantic or definitional but are about the very philosophy and principles on which systems of juvenile justice are based – there are a number of general trends which can be identified in relation to offending by children and young people in Europe (see Asquith 1992b for a fuller statement of trends in delinquency in Europe and in particular in Scotland, England and Wales, Sweden and Holland).

A number of trends can be identified in statistics referring to offending by children and young people in Europe (Junger-Tas 1991, 1994). In particular:

1. Juvenile delinquency is essentially a male phenomenon and juvenile justice systems deal largely with male offenders.
2. From the Second World War until the mid-1980s, there was a general increase in crime with increases in offending by children and young people particularly notable.
3. There has since the mid-1980s been a general reduction in the volume of delinquency in most Western European countries for both boys and girls.
4. The great majority of offences committed by children and young people are less serious property offences.
5. There has been a reduction in property offences and theft with most notable decreases in relation to offences such as shoplifting, burglary and handling stolen goods.
6. There has been an increase in the number of serious offences of violence against the person.
7. There has a quantitative change in the levels of involvement of girls, and even in relation to the offences where there has been a general decrease, the decrease has been less marked for girls than for boys. In qualitative terms, girls and young women are becoming increasingly involved in drug-related and fraud offence behaviour.
8. Disproportionate numbers of non-nationals and members of ethnic minorities appear in the official crime and prison statistics.

Explaining delinquency

The trends in delinquency since the Second World War can be explained in a number of ways. What is less easy to explain is which factors can be employed to account for delinquent behaviour as such. In what follows, some of the reasons for these very broad trends will be identified prior to considering what implications they may have for our attempts to understand and explain offending by children and young people, and for attempts to develop appropriate delinquency prevention measures.

Accounting for the trends in delinquency

Demographic changes

The decrease in delinquency rates throughout Europe can in part be attributed to demographic changes; in particular to the reduction of the population at the ages which directly concern us. Conversely, the increase in delinquency in the 1960s and 1970s could be explained partly by the increased number of children reaching their teenage years as a result of the post-war baby boom. But there is a problem with this in as much as it cannot explain the reduction in delinquency overall. In real terms the numbers have gone down, but more importantly, the rate of delinquency behaviour has also gone down in the past few years. There are two questions which then have to be posed. One is how can we account for the increased delinquency of the 1960s and 1970s by factors additional to the 'baby boom' variable. The other is how can we explain the decrease in delinquency in absolute terms and also in the rate of delinquency since 1984 onwards. The assumption made here is that demographic factors themselves cannot account for such changes.

Social changes

In relation to the first question there are a number of explanations which can be offered. Explanations for the growth in crime generally until the mid 1980s cited, for example by Sarnecki (1989), are the increased availability of consumer goods and also the changing structure of shopping facilities. However, whereas this might account for the increase in crime overall, it cannot explain the larger increase in criminal behaviour by the young, which occurred until 1984–5.

A number of alternative explanations have been offered. *Increased prosperity* has of course made available a range of goods which are small but also of considerable value and which can account for the increased theft by delinquents. Both Junger-Tas (1991) and Sarnecki (1991) point to the significance of thefts from and theft of cars in the crime statistics for this period and the general availability of both opportunities and targets for theft by children and young people. The general relationship between delinquency and periods of economic affluence is referred to by Sarnecki as *'welfare criminality'*.

In addition, studies have identified the importance of *the lack of supervision and control* on such objects. Cohen and Felson (in Junger-Tas 1991) claim that the period up till the late Seventies at least was characterised by the ready availability of consumer goods in new shopping arrangements with little developed protection or security strategies.

Perhaps the most widely posited explanation for the increase relates to the position of young people in society and *to changing relationships between children and parents, and also to changing relationships between the young and the labour market.*

Again, Junger-Tas (1991) and Sarnecki (1991) allude to the importance of changing socialisation patterns in promoting delinquent behaviour. Both refer to the breakdown in or at least the altered patterns of informal social control exercised by parents over children and the increased importance attached to associations and friendships with peers. What is clearly the case is that increasing attention has been paid more recently to the role of the family either in inhibiting the development of those risk factors associated with delinquency, or in failing to insulate children from them. In general the significance of the family is reflected in the increasing resort to explanations of offending by children and young people which centre on the family and family break-up and the way in which many practices, measures and policies are now driven by family centre concerns (Harris 1989; Utting *et al.* 1993; Melton 1995). For example, the time spent with parents and in the family home was much less than just after the Second World War. Sarnecki's work shows that young people of 15, 16 and 17 spent as much as five to six hours each day with their friends away from parental supervision.

In addition, Sarnecki (1991) again attributes much of the delinquency of this period to the changing role of the young in society generally, describing their *transition from a producer's role to a consumer role.* Again, the strain that this produces for the young is considerable, bearing in mind that the encouragement to act as a consumer is not always matched by the availability of legitimate means to procure goods.

What also has to be recognised is that as Asquith (1992a) has argued, many young people and not just offenders experience what can be called *a politics of exclusion*. By a politics of exclusion is meant the inability of many young people to actively participate in mainstream social life (**Bailleau** develops the implications of marginalisation and exclusion of the young in Chapter 2). And at a time when acknowledgement is given in a number of countries in Europe and elsewhere to the widening of the gap between the rich and the poor and to the creation of what has become known as an underclass, many of our young will experience all the hallmarks of poverty with the marginalisation and exclusion that this produces.

But in explaining the *decrease* since the mid-1980s, the explanations that are available are a mirror image of those just considered. In particular, there is evidence to support the argument that children have, since the mid-1980s, been subject to much closer supervision and control than children in the period from the Second World War on. Controls have been exercised in a number of ways and these include:

- greater supervision of children in schools and in the family
- greater supervision and control in the community. In particular, the development of crime prevention strategies, neighbourhood watch schemes and the acceptance of a target hardening approach have served to reduce the ready availability of easily stolen goods.

According to Barclay and Turner (1991) the dramatic reduction in shoplifting was attributed by Chief Constables in England to a number of factors, amongst which were closer policing, surveillance strategies and electronic devices, including city centre surveillance cameras. But they also explained the reduction by reference to other considerations such as the social crime prevention programmes developed in a number of areas and also to the diversion of offenders from the juvenile court system. Pierre de Liege (1991) would also claim that the reduction in crime and delinquency since 1985–6 could also be explained by the adoption of prevention strategies based on a philosophy of social crime prevention.

Once again, to repeat a point made above, the reason for referring to the measures and strategies employed to deal with delinquency is that such measures will in themselves have a significant impact on just what profile delinquency takes in specific countries at specific points in time.

Changing conceptions of delinquency

The other reason for alluding to measures taken to deal with delinquency is that they are all based on a certain set of assumptions about the nature of delinquency. How we conceive of delinquency will in part dictate what we do about it. Not only has there been quantitative change in the volume of delinquency since the Second World War, but in Western Europe there have been changes in the very conception of delinquency itself. In particular there has been a gradual shift away from individualistic explanations of delinquency as either a behaviour that is punishable or as a behaviour that can be explained by factors in the delinquents. Testimony to this is the move to raise the age at which juveniles can be dealt with in the juvenile justice system.

Moreover, there is increasing recognition of the need to see the young offender not in isolation from his position in the social, economic and political structure. Recent policies, particularly those based on a social crime prevention philosophy, have recognised the need to view the offender in the context of social life generally and have therefore been based on a multi sectoral and multi agency approach. There has also been concern expressed that official government policies may well in themselves influence the profile of those involved in delinquent behaviour.

But just as explanations of offending by children and young people have shifted, so too is there in the research literature evidence of a shift in the acceptance of and validity of particular kinds of approaches to dealing with children and young people who offend. These too are of particular significance for any attempt to devise appropriate strategies for prevention, in particular, the recognition of the importance of early year intervention in the lives of children at risk; the concern with the persistent and serious young offender; and the search for a new paradigm of justice for children and young people.

Offending by children and young people[2]

A number of themes recur frequently in the literature relating to offending by children and young people, all of which have important

2 I am grateful to my colleagues, Maureen Buist, Cathlin McCauley, Nicola Loughran and Michael Montgomery, on the project *A Review of Children, Young People and Offending in Scotland* undertaken for The Scottish Office (McCauley 1995) and on which this section of the Introduction draws. This section in particular draws on the section of the report contributed by Nicola Loughran.

implications for the development of systems of juvenile justice and for relevant measures and programmes. The following is a summary of the most important of these recurring findings and recommendations and covers:

1. The early years
2. Drug use and crime
3. Persistent and serious young offenders
4. Girls, women and crime
5. Offending and ethnic minority youth
6. Punishment and incarceration
7. Successful interventions
8. Social crime prevention
9. Fragmentation of policies
10. The search for a new conception of juvenile justice

1. *The early years* – Within the very first years of birth there are clear warning signs, evident in both the psychological and physical development of the child, of anti-social and troublesome behaviour (see Farrington 1994a,b,c; Farrington and Wikström 1994; Farrington *et al.* 1994). The early identification of high-risk factors is not difficult for parents and teachers.

    Similarly, there is clear evidence of continuity in problematic behaviour: aggressive/anti-social behaviour in young children often predicts later more aggressive, violent and delinquent behaviour. High-risk factors such as hyperactivity; high impulsivity; low intelligence; poor parental child management; parental neglect; offending parents and siblings; early child-bearing (teenage pregnancy); deprived background, for example, low-income mother dependent on state welfare assistance; absent father; maternal substance use in pregnancy – associated with low birth-weight babies/psychological disorders/perinatal complications – are all associated with aggressive, problematic and later delinquent behaviour in the child. Such factors are cumulative and tend to coincide.

    The difficulties encountered in the early years may also be compounded considerably by the experience of poverty and disadvantage and the literature does identify a close relationship between crime, poverty and disadvantage. The impact of the parenting role in the context of disadvantage is highlighted as a crucial variable.

However, the adverse effects of many of these high-risk factors appear to be negated or diluted, in some instances, by the presence of certain positive factors. The 'insulatory' effect of a 'good home' environment such as warm, supportive social/family networks has been noted to be able to counter the effects of perinatal complications, hyperactivity and low socio-economic status. Parents of young delinquents typically 'use' either one of two extreme styles of parenting: either harsh and authoritarian, or passive and neglectful. Poor parental supervision and the absence of clear communication of expectations and acceptable norms of behaviour by parents also typified the families of young offenders.

Parent-training programmes and intervention at the earliest possible stage to break the cycle of troublesome behaviour is, therefore, advocated (a theme which Bright addresses in Chapter 1). What the literature suggests is that the later the intervention, the less chance of changing child and parental behaviour. The role of the paediatrician has been cited as crucial. Health advisers are in the unique position of being able to recognise and intervene in cases of neglectful/harmful parenting which have been shown to be linked with child behaviour problems and have proved successful in reducing instances of child neglect and cruelty.

The link between low IQ and aggressive and troublesome behaviour appears to persist into the school years, later leading to truancy, exclusion from school and a range of delinquent activities. Good pre-school education such as the Perry/Head-Start model presents a cost-effective way of raising educational achievement, attendance and standards of behaviour in children throughout the school years and a reduction in delinquency. Such pre-school provision targeted at high-risk populations, augmented with parental skills training or family intervention programmes focusing on the social, psychological, physical and educational development of children, can make a substantial impact on lowering the need for special educational placements later on; on levels of parental mismanagement; on conduct problems in children and consequently juvenile delinquency.

The range and nature of problematic behaviours identifiable in troublesome pre-school children typically persist and worsen on reaching school. These 'multiple at risk' characteristics and 'warning signs' include: dishonesty; daring; lack of concentration; restlessness; hyperactivity; impulsivity; low IQ. Delinquent and low-achieving children tend to group together, indulging in higher levels of drug use, offending, anti-authoritarian attitudes and police contacts. But removing such children from mainstream schooling stigmatises, labels and removes them from the normalising influence of their peers. Pupils' behaviour may improve while 'off-site', but the problems which precipitated their removal are left unaddressed, which can result in repetition of the offending behaviour on return to class/school. Multi-disciplinary support teams composed of welfare, special educational and psychological advisers have been suggested as an alternative.

Dealing with the troublesome pupil within the class, with special support, if possible is urged. Delinquency, low school achievement, truancy and consequent school exclusion tend to coincide. The school is very often the 'gatekeeper' to more formal criminal justice measures. Schools which encourage all pupils, regardless of educational capability, to work in 'partnership' with their teachers and parents in their personal educational attainment tend to have lower rates of truancy, make lower recourse to exclusions and encounter far less serious pupil behaviour problems.

2. *Drug use and crime* – The frequency of delinquent activity and drug use appears to be inter-correlated. There appears to be a host of duplicate factors which tend to propel children into involvement in both crime and drugs, such as lack of conventional attachments to family/school; and attachment, instead, to delinquent and substance abusing friends. Conventional attachments can be weakened by disruptive/inadequate parenting/poverty/learning disabilities/emotional disorders and periods in care.

Characteristics of young drug abusers include low socio-economic or deprived background/unemployment/ exclusion from school/low educational achievement and boredom.

Although there is no direct link between drugs and crime, the establishment of one habit tends to worsen both. Since drugs and crime appear to be encouraged in the same circles, strengthening of conventional supports, such as ties with family and 'normal' peer groups is urged. The need to avoid stigmatisation is also stressed. Treatment programmes must take account of long-term social and economic backgrounds of the young abusers including issues of poverty, homelessness and/or boredom. Substance use is intimately linked to culture and, in some circles, criminality. The best strategy, therefore, is prevention of commencement of drug-taking and crime. The encouragement of sports and education in the harmful effects of drugs at school, and thereby healthy lifestyles, is advocated. Otherwise, education in harm-reduction is urged, that is, how to take drugs safely and without dependence.

3. *Persistent and serious young offenders* – A very large proportion of crime does appear to be committed by a very small number of juvenile delinquents. Persistent young offenders engage in the same range of criminal activities as less prolific young offenders, but do so more often. Characteristics and family backgrounds of 'chronics' mirror that of young offenders in general – only the nature of their problems appear to be worse and more numerous, the characteristics more pronounced. IQ and family income tend to be lower, parental mismanagement even more authoritarian or neglectful.

   The syndrome of anti-social behaviour in persistent young offenders tends to commence earlier, persist and become particularly acute. Substance use is higher, delinquent friends more numerous and troublesome. They tend to have more pronounced educational difficulties, particularly in reading; to co-offend with similar peers, truant and leave school earlier – very often through exclusion. What did appear uniquely to characterise the background of so many persistent young offenders was the abundance of chaotic, traumatic experiences such as personal victimisation, deaths, accidents and suicides of close family and friends.

Persistent young offenders tend to be well known by social services – but more often have come to their attention through social/welfare problems, not for their offending. Their level of emotional disorders is exceedingly high – including distress, depression, anger, etc. The reasons young offenders *per se* give for getting involved in crime consistently are: for material/financial motives primarily, then boredom and excitement. Reasons for stopping include: 'growing up' and the positive influences of family – especially mothers, girlfriends and grandmothers. Surprisingly, young offenders appear to hold conventional long-term aspirations – to 'settle down with family' and find work.

With regard to those children and young people who commit the more serious offences, what has been illustrated clearly by cases such as the James Bulger case is the severe tension that exists in any criminal justice system between dealing with children as being vulnerable and in need of care (even when they commit particularly serious offences), and a reaction which involves dealing with them as rational responsible individuals who should experience the whole gamut of the criminal trial and be deemed deserving and worthy of punishment. The Prime Minister's statement after the Bulger case that as a society 'we need to understand less and condemn more' crystallises neatly the tension between sharply contrasting philosophies. What this also highlights is what can be referred to as the 'twin track' approach in which for the majority of cases of offending by children and young people involving (as we have seen earlier in this chapter) less serious property offences, there is a commitment to dealing with such offenders as far as possible in terms of their personal, familial or social needs. For those who commit the more serious offences the trend in Europe is to adopt a more justice and punitive based approach with court appearance as part of the whole process of dealing with the case. That is a characteristic of all European systems of juvenile justice. **McGhee *et al.*** in Chapter 3 and **Graham** in Chapter 4 both outline very different systems for dealing with children and young people who offend, and what is apparent in both contributions is the tension experienced in *all,* without exception, systems of juvenile justice – that between measures devised to meet the needs of the majority of offenders (who as we have seen tend to commit the less serious offences) and the appropriate measures for dealing with those who commit the more serious types of offences. In many respects, the 'twin-track' approach referred to above is expressed in all systems of juvenile justice, though exactly how it is expressed varies greatly from system to system. The merit of considering the juvenile justice systems of Scotland and England and Wales is that it crystallises the difficulty of resolving the conflict between dealing with less serious offenders on the one hand and the more serious cases on the other. The uniqueness of the Scottish system of juvenile justice can be best appreciated in comparison with other systems. In addition the comparison between what happens in Scotland and in England and Wales serves to emphasise forcefully just how different the two countries are in the way in which offending by children and young people is responded to.

The evidence from **Garbarino and Kostelny** in Chapter 5 is that there has been a dramatic increase in the United States in the number of offences involving the deaths of children and teenagers at the hands of other young people. The growth in offences involving severe violence against the person by young people prompts Garbarino and Kostelny to compare the experiences of many American children to those of children in the war zone. Whereas a consideration of the profile of crime and offending by children and young people throughout Europe does suggest that crime overall is decreasing, or at the very least the rate of increase has slowed down, it is the social and political reaction to the small group of children who commit very serious offences involving violence which influences disproportionately the direction juvenile justice systems may take. In that respect, **Garbarino and Kostelny's** chapter is highly relevant both in the warning they give of how youth crime might develop in this country and in the problems posed for any system of juvenile justice in devising appropriate means for dealing with such children.

4. *Girls, women and crime* – What is also clear from the literature is that there is very little material relating to offending by girls and young women, though it does appear to be the case that, reflecting the increasing involvement of girls in specific areas of crime such as drugs and fraud, this will become an important aspect of criminological and penological work in the future. But the relevance of the relative 'invisibility' of girls and women in the literature does mirror the fact that explanations of crime and offending are generally based on attempts to explain crime by males and that the measures devised for dealing with offending behaviour are, by the same token, by and large designed for males.

   What has to be asked is whether, if the assumptions about offending and how to deal with it are based on male stereotypes, measures and programmes for females are in turn based on legitimate and appropriate assumptions. In Chapter 6, **Samuel and Tisdall** challenge particular conceptions of female criminality and review the relevance of a number of theoretical positions on women and crime by considering available official statistics. They argue that much more work, particularly of a qualitative nature, is required to further our general understanding of those factors which may be used to account for criminal behaviour in general though their main focus is of course on women and girls. But on the basis of their own work they are able to argue from their consideration of the official statistics that there is evidence of leniency shown to women, which can be associated with the notion of chivalry which appears in the literature. But further work is required for a more comprehensive analysis.

5. *Offending and ethnic minority youth* – What is clear from a search of the literature is just how little work has been done in relation to offending and ethnic minority youth either in detailing the way in which crime and offending behaviour is experienced by young people from the ethnic minorities, or how they perceive their own involvement in offending behaviour or indeed the way in which their behaviour is policed. Just as there is a desperate need for more systematic research to be done with regard to girls and young women, so too is our knowledge

about the particular situation of ethnic minority youth particularly weak.

The work done by Anderson *et al.* (1990) on the experience of offending by young people in Scotland, and the review of youth centred surveys of young people's lifestyles by McCauley (1995), both illustrate this particular gap in the literature. Hunter's work (1995) in researching the crime experiences of young people from ethnic minorities is a welcome contribution but one that has to be supplemented by further work in this field.

6. *Punishment and incarceration* – Punishment and incarceration have a negative effect on recidivism. The most successful criminal justice interventions appear to be employment-focused programmes. Multi-modal cognitive-behavioural projects such as social skills training and aggression reduction techniques have also reduced problematic behaviours. Intensive Treatment (I.T.) for youth at risk, supporting youth within their communities using multi-agency resources, for example, social work, community education and schools, has been received positively.

   The literature suggests the inappropriateness of custodial intervention and indeed further – that it may be counterproductive. This of course reflects an increasing commitment to reducing the use made of custodial or residential facilities manifested throughout Europe (Asquith 1995), and to the actual reduction in the numbers and rates of child and young offenders sent to residential facilities and custodial programmes. In Chapter 8, **Littlewood** provides comprehensive analysis of the use made of secure accommodation concentrating in particular on what happens to those under 16 or 17 in the context of custody in Britain. He reviews the criteria used for the placement of children in secure units, the sorts of children sent to them, the policies of such units, the treatment practices and the preparation and activities of their staff. What **Littlewood** questions is whether a defence can be made of the practice of placing children who have not committed serious offences in secure units, even where their function is supposedly care. Certainly, the whole thrust of movements in Europe is that this is clearly wrong and that the use of custodial care for any offender should be used only as a last resort.

7. *Successful interventions* – Vital components of successful intervention include: relating to the nature of young offenders' problems, for example, truancy, running away, substance abuse, social skills; diversion away from formal measures whenever possible (the role of the Reporters in Scotland is particularly important); avoidance of net-widening; removal of offenders from employment and accommodation; the need for maximum clarity of focus in objectives, methods and expectation of programmes.

   The extension of I.T. type provisions to the 16–18-year-old age group (singled out as falling between the Hearing system and the Courts) has been recommended in many reports though the lack of community placements for girls has been criticised. In Chapter 7, **Robertson and McClintock** draw a number of conclusions about the merits of I.T., arguing that it is clear that 'I.T. can greatly facilitate the diversion of youngsters from more severe penal measures, although the existence of I.T. projects is not *per se* sufficient to ensure this' (p.149). **Robertson and McClintock** make no strong claim that I.T. is any more effective than other measures, but argue that since it is no less effective and given that it appears to enjoy the confidence of parents, children and professionals there are good grounds for continuing to develop I.T. as an appropriate and less intrusive form of initiative.

8. *Social crime prevention* – Social crime prevention advocates stress the critical need to address the social and economic contexts in which crime flourishes. Scotland's Hearing System is applauded for its welfare and comprehensive approach to dealing with young offenders. But wider consideration of the effects of youth policies on the life chances of young people is overdue. Crime prevention strategies must also address the lack of employment, training, and housing and the dearth of realistic prospects for young people becoming financially independent.

In later chapters in this book, both **Bright** (Chapter 1) and **Bailleau** (Chapter 2) develop these very themes, advocating that prevention policies be multi-faceted, involving a combination of central government, local government, community and voluntary agency initiatives. It is clear from the literature and from the arguments made by **Bright** and **Bailleau** that the marginalisation and deprivation of many young people can only be meaningfully tackled through such comprehensive strategies in an attempt not simply to reduce crime and delinquency but more broadly to enhance their life opportunities.

This can only be achieved, at the local level through addressing the social and welfare difficulties and under-privileged backgrounds of many young offenders, and through inter-agency co-operation between all key players – police, judiciary, social services and community, as exemplified by Safer City initiatives. The preservation of links with family and community is always paramount. There is a pressing need to persist and persevere with working with the most at-risk and excluded sections of society – very often the most difficult to reach and work with.

9. *Fragmentation of policies* – The fragmentation at both local and national level of policies, agencies and initiatives relating to crime, children and the family must inevitably be less effective than a more comprehensive children and youth care policy. What the literature identifies is the need for continuity of provision, integrating the voluntary sector. Crime prevention, to be effective, should ideally be an aspect of mainstream policies. Local multi-agency forums are needed to plan multi-faceted strategies covering poverty; pre-school provision; education; parenting; family support; employment; training, etc. Priority areas should be identified in order to target cost-effectively high-risk populations with high-risk children. There is also a general lack of involvement and consultation with young people on their perceptions of their needs.

   In terms of policy, therefore, the main thrust of what is clearly discernible in the literature is that crime prevention strategies must operate not merely as criminal justice reactions, but include also a range of early-years health and education initiatives to counter the high-risk precursors of delinquent behaviour. Farrington (1994a, p.30) has highlighted some of the most successful programmes and identifies a new role for a traditional support service provided for families with new-born children:

> Health visitors are among the most important health professionals (community nurses) who routinely provide services to young mothers and their infants in their homes. In the light of the American home-visiting experiments, it is plausible to suggest that a more intensive home visiting programme, with small caseloads, might be successful in reducing hyperactivity, school failure, child conduct problems and ultimately delinquency and crime. Intensive health visiting programmes might be even more effective if they were supplemented by parent management training and pre-school intellectual enrichment programmes.

Now whether preventive work can be centred around the activities of such as health visitors is of course an issue to be debated. However, what Farrington does highlight by making the suggestion is that a reorientation of the availability of resources away from the criminal justice system to measures which target early year experiences might be a more productive and effective means of reducing crime and offending by children and young people in the long term.

Only by developing and promoting strategies which focus on the family, social and community environment of young people can the factors which anticipate (and indeed predict) delinquent, criminal and other behaviours be meaningfully dealt with. A policy of crime prevention, on the basis of this argument, which ignores the potential for change through affecting the social and community environment in which children and young people experience their daily lives will inevitably fail.

10. *The search for a new conception of juvenile justice* – The history of juvenile justice is one which is characterised by a pendulum-like swing between the merits of a welfare approach to dealing with

> children and young people who commit offences and an approach based on a more traditional crime, responsibility, punishment philosophy (often referred to in the literature as a 'justice' approach). What is also clear from the research literature is that fundamental questions are being asked as to whether these two philosophies are the only relevant framework on which to base the principles of a system of justice for dealing with young offenders.

In Chapter 9, **Walgrave** critically reviews the principles on which a number of European systems of juvenile justice are based and in particular questions whether it might not be time to move on from the traditional dichotomy between welfare and traditional justice models as a basis for dealing with children and young people who offend. He advocates consideration being given to a new model of 'restorative' justice which has evolved gradually from the philosophies on which schemes such as mediation and reparation initiatives are based.

The chapters in this book were chosen with the need to address current issues in the development of policies for dealing with children and young people who offend. Some are based on empirical research, whereas others reflect the current preoccupation with the questioning of the fundamental principles on which systems of juvenile justice are, or should be, based. In that respect they all make a direct and relevant contribution to contemporary debate about, and review of, the most appropriate measures and policies for dealing with children and young people who offend. The particularly international nature of some of the contributions reflects the fact that the issues considered are by no means exclusive to the United Kingdom. The hope is that the contents of the specific chapters in this book will help others to take forward some of the key issues in what is, in reference to the development of measures to deal with young offenders, an ongoing process.

References

Anderson, S. (1994) *The Scottish Crime Survey*. Edinburgh: HMSO.

Anderson, S., Kinsey, R. and Smith, C. (1990) *Cautionary Tales: A Study of Young People and Crime in Edinburgh*. Centre for Criminology, University of Edinburgh.

Asquith, S. (1992a) Coming of age: 21 years of the Scottish Children's Hearings System. *Journal of Scottish Affairs*. Scottish Government

Yearbook, Unit for the Study of Government in Scotland, Edinburgh, 157–172.

Asquith, S. (1992b) *The Evolution of Juvenile Justice in Western Europe.* Strasbourg: Council of Europe.

Asquith, S. (1995a) *Analysis of Provisions for Young Offenders in Member States of the Council of Europe.* Strasbourg: Council of Europe.

Asquith, S. (1995b) Children, crime and society. In M. Hill and J. Aldgate (eds) *Child Welfare Services.* London: Jessica Kingsley Publishers.

Barclay, G. and Turner, D. (1991) Recent trends in official statistics on juvenile offending in England and Wales. In T. Booth (ed.) *Juvenile Justice in the New Europe.* Sheffield: Social Services Monographs.

Cappelaere, G. (1995) *Children's Rights and Juvenile Justice.* Paper presented at conference on International Rights of the Child. Sion, Switzerland: Kurt Bosch Institute.

Dunkel, F. (1991) Legal differences in juvenile criminology in Europe. In T. Booth (ed) *Juvenile Justice in the New Europe.* Sheffield: Social Services Monographs.

Farrington, D.P. (1994a) Early developmental prevention of juvenile delinquency. *Journal of the Royal Society for the Promotion of Arts and Commerce,* November, 22–34.

Farrington, D.P. (1994b) Delinquency prevention in the first few years of life: Part 1. *Journal of the Peace and Local Government Law 158,* 33, 531.

Farrington, D.P. (1994c) *Later Life Outcomes of Truants in the Cambridge Study.* Department of Criminology, Cambridge University.

Farrington, D.P. and Wikström, P.H. (1994) *Changes in Crime and Crime Prevention, Annual Review.* Oslo/Stockholm: Scandinavian University Press.

Farrington, D., Langan, P.A. and Wikström, P.H. (1994) Changes in crime and punishment in America, England and Sweden between 1980s and 1990s. *Studies on Crime and Crime Prevention Annual Review, Oslo/Stockholm, Scandinavian University Press 3,* 104–130.

Harris, R. (1989) *Suffer the Children: The Family, the State and the Social Worker.* Hull: Hull University Press.

Hunter, M. (1995) *Ethnic Minority Young People and Crime.* University of Glasgow: Centre for the Study of the Child and Society.

Junger-Tas, J. (1991) 'Juvenile and petty crime in the 21st century.' In J. Junger-Tas and I. Sagel-Grande (eds) *Criminology in the 21st Century.* Leuven: Garant.

Junger-Tas, J. (1994) Delinquent behaviour among young people in the Western World. Research Paper, Ministry of Justice, Amsterdam.

Junger-Tas, J. and Sagel-Grande, I. (eds) (1991) *Criminology in the 21st Century. A Collection of Essays presented to Wouter Buikhuisen*. Leuven: Garant.

McCauley, C. (1995) The lifestyles and experiences of Scottish youth. In S. Asquith, M. Buist, C. McCauley, N. Loughran and M. Montgomery (eds) *A Review of Children, Young People and Offending in Scotland*. Edinburgh: The Scottish Office.

Melton, G. (ed.) (1995) *The Individual, the Family and Social Good: Personal Fulfilment in Times of Change. Current Theory and Research in Motivation*. Nebraska: University of Nebraska.

Pierre de Liege, M. (1991) Social development and the prevention of crime in France. In F. Heidensohn and M. Farrell (eds) *Crime in Europe*. London: Routledge.

Sarnecki, J. (1989) *Juvenile Delinquency in Sweden: An Overview*. Stockholm: National Crime Prevention Council.

Sarnecki, J. (1991) Reactions to crimes committed by young people. In A. Snare (ed.) *Youth, Crime and Justice*. Oxford: Norwegian University Press.

Utting, D., Bright, J. and Henricson, C. (1993) *Crime and the Family: Improving Child-Rearing and Preventing Delinquency*. London: Family Policy Studies Centre.

Chapter 1

Preventing Youth Crime in High Crime Areas

Towards a Strategy[1]

Jon Bright

Introduction

In this chapter, a strategy will be proposed for reducing the impact and level of youth crime. It will consider (briefly) the national policy context, propose a methodology for addressing the problem at a local level and suggest a preventive framework that can be applied to high crime locations. Its theme is prevention rather than rehabilitation. It will therefore concentrate on primary and secondary prevention (through strengthening the crime prevention capacity of community institutions) rather than on preventing reoffending by convicted young offenders (through the criminal justice system).

It is now widely accepted that problems of youth crime and anti-social behaviour are unlikely to be resolved satisfactorily through criminal justice policy. Research from many countries suggests that the formal processes of the criminal justice system – apprehending, prosecuting, sentencing, punishing and rehabilitating offenders – are not an effective means of controlling crime (Graham 1990). Their principal function is to react to the relatively small proportion of crime that comes to their attention and process the very small number of offenders who get caught (Home Office 1993a).

This perspective has been reflected in Government policy since 1984. Successive circulars and guidance have stressed the important

---

1 This chapter was first prepared for the 22nd Cropwood Round Table Conference on 14–16 September 1994 at Robinson College, Cambridge: 'Preventing crime and disorder: targeting strategies and community responsibilities'.

contribution agencies outside the criminal justice system can make to preventing crime through participation in local multi-agency partnerships of which there are now close to 200 in existence in the UK (although since 1992, there has been a renewed focus on controlling crime through the criminal justice system).

Yet it was only in 1993 that detailed guidance was issued on what partnerships might do and how they might do it (Home Office 1993b). The emphasis given to multi-agency activity has appeared to downplay the role of action by single agencies in spite of the fact that most crime prevention action is undertaken by agencies acting individually or bilaterally. Furthermore, the work of many crime prevention partnerships has been insufficiently focused or rigorous and there have been very few successful evaluations. The 'partnership approach' is claimed everywhere to be a success but, in truth, it has not yet adequately demonstrated the benefits of prevention. This situation has had a number of consequences for the continuing debate about crime and young people.

First, political and public debate on youth crime is still relatively uninformed and characterised by calls for more discipline in the home and the school, and tougher action by the criminal justice agencies. This does not advance the field very far because it is largely exhortatory. Second, the UK dedicates well under 1 per cent of its criminal justice budget to prevention and does not have any kind of national prevention strategy. It is not alone; most other countries (apart from some in northern Europe) are in the same position (House of Commons, Canada 1993). Third, there is little agreement amongst policy makers about the scale of youth crime, its relative seriousness or how it might be prevented. Finally, the lack of agreement over what should be done to prevent criminality results, by default, in a heavy emphasis on situational crime prevention. In spite of the maturity and sophistication of the situational approach (Clarke 1994), it is not seen by many as a sufficient response to anti-social behaviour and youth crime.

Youth offending and social policy

Local strategies to address youth crime problems operate, of course, within a policy context determined by central government. Government can seek to influence levels of offending directly by promoting more preventive work by the police and other criminal justice agencies. Examples might include 'problem oriented' community policing, such as that pioneered by some American police forces; or intensive community-based programmes for persistent young offenders on the lines of the 'Youth at Risk' initiative, again an American import.

Government can also influence levels of offending indirectly through mainstream social policies such as those concerned with the family, education, housing, training and employment. Such policies can strengthen or weaken the capacity of the family and community institutions to socialise and supervise the young. They can also assist or impede the difficult transition from adolescence to adulthood and maturity. They can therefore impact positively or negatively on those most likely to offend.

For example, in the UK, education policy has promoted competition between schools. This makes it less likely that schools will wish to accommodate troublesome young people who are, as a result, more likely to fail school and drift into crime. Now government may consider that this is an acceptable cost to pay, when compared to the benefits brought about for the majority by increased competition. But at least it might have considered, at the time, how this unwelcome side effect could have been avoided.

It is government's response to changing economic circumstances and labour markets which many consider to be one of the most important issues in the debate about youth crime. In many parts of the USA, UK and Europe, the decline of unskilled and semi-skilled work has resulted in unemployed young men growing up to feel that they have no stake in society. This has obvious implications for offending. Criminal activity declines with age when young men acquire a personal stake in conformity (through marriage and employment) and the risks of crime outweigh the rewards (Hope 1993, pp.104–108 and 151–156). The failure of low-skilled young men to enter permanently into the job market reduces their stake in conformity.

It also means that they are less likely to lead a stable life. Family formation and finding a place in a community brings rewards and obligations. If this opportunity is not available, there is little incentive for young men to grow out of crime or lose a taste for disorder. This is damaging both to them and their communities. Creating training and employment opportunities must therefore be a key feature of a national strategy that seeks to reduce crime and criminality. Similarly, some research suggests that homelessness and poor or temporary housing increases the likelihood of young people offending, a problem that is also best addressed through a national strategy (Wilkinson 1993).

Government policy, therefore, creates the context in which local efforts will be more or less successful. Because offending is susceptible to influence by so many factors, interdepartmental coordination is necessary to ensure that government policies take crime and criminality prevention into account as a matter of course (Home Affairs Select Committee 1993).

The remainder of this chapter will consider how crime prevention might be planned and managed at a local level.

Planning prevention: towards a methodology

In order to ensure a more consistent approach to prevention, the Home Office has issued guidance on how to develop a local crime prevention programme (Home Office 1993b). Such programmes may be developed by multi-agency partnerships or by agencies, acting alone or bilaterally. It advocates a methodology which can be applied to most situations in which crime (including youth crime) is a problem. This might be in a residential area, a city centre, a school, a shopping mall, or an industrial area. There are four stages:

- defining the problem
- deciding what to do
- implementing the programme
- assessing what has been achieved.

Although this may seem obvious, such a systematic approach is rare in the crime prevention field. Problems are not always *defined* precisely, options rarely *appraised* carefully, insufficient thought is given to the *process* of implementation and activity is rarely *evaluated*. Each of these stages will now be dealt with briefly.

Defining the problem

The first stage is to define the problem. This is done by means of an audit. A crime audit involves assembling available crime, offender and victim data, consulting agencies and residents and reviewing existing practice. This process will identify the scale, impact and cost of each crime-related problem and enable decisions about priorities to be made. It is especially important to consult young people. They will have much to say about crime and its prevention, not least because they witness three times more crime than adults and are therefore a good source of information (Kinsey 1993). They will also want to be involved in developing solutions. The purpose of the audit is not only to obtain information about crime. It is a participative exercise which ensures that the problem is shared, resources mobilised and solutions owned by a wide range of agencies and interests. This is important for the success of multi-agency work.

Deciding what to do

Having defined the problem and identified priorities, it is necessary to decide what to do. Options can be appraised, research findings considered and a package of measures prepared for the area in question. It is important to be sure that what is being proposed is actually going to impact on the problem. It is not enough to hope that it will. A greater degree of certainty is necessary. This can be achieved by clarifying the *mechanism* by which the option will impact on the problem, the *outcome* that is sought and the *conditions* necessary for the mechanism to work (Tilley 1993). For example, the problem may be anti-social behaviour by young people. The proposed solution is more police patrols. Skilled policing may be able to help reduce the level of anti-social behaviour (outcome) by imposing boundaries on behaviour and drawing attention to alternative activities (mechanism). This may only work, however, if a team of dedicated community police officers is assigned to the area on a permanent basis (condition).

But this may not be possible. What is on offer is an extra six hours patrolling a week by various officers. It may be judged that under these conditions, the mechanism to achieve the outcome would not be triggered and that another option should be considered. Rigorous appraisal of this kind should be applied to social crime prevention measures such as family support and youth crime prevention projects if they are to win wider support and be treated as seriously as situational prevention.

Implementing the programme

Crime is a multi-dimensional problem. It therefore demands multi-dimensional solutions. These are difficult to operationalise for a variety of reasons that have been discussed elsewhere (see Tilley 1993, pp.12–13). Difficulties are most likely to occur when addressing problems such as family stress and youth disaffection which are *no one agency's primary responsibility*. The solution is not only better coordination, as is often thought. The problems caused as a result of dispersed responsibility, differential perceptions of the problem or a lack of will to act can only be satisfactorily addressed by assigning *leadership* of the multi-agency initiative to a senior person in the agency with the biggest stake in the area.

Their role will be to (a) address those priority issues that are clearly not the remit of any one agency or even sector (the most obvious concern preventive work with families, children and young people); (b) obtain commitment from the various agencies, set clear and achievable targets and monitor their implementation; and (c) exercise leadership, coordinate activity, lobby for resources, identify gaps in provision and opportunities for funding, think strategically and 'make things happen' (Bright 1993, p.48).

Assessing achievement

It is important to monitor performance for two reasons. First, those managing initiatives need to know whether they are working or not. Second, funders want to see evidence of effectiveness. Crime prevention initiatives should have an evaluation plan. With assistance, monitoring progress can be undertaken by projects themselves. External evaluation is of great benefit if resources are available. In the UK, far too little support in terms of both advice and finance is available to evaluate initiatives.

Youth crime: a preventive framework

Having discussed how crime prevention might be planned, this chapter will now discuss how youth crime might be prevented. A model is proposed that involves two sets of measures: *those which make crime more difficult to commit* and *those that address the inclination of young people to offend*. In high crime areas, both approaches are usually needed.

The left hand column in the diagram is reasonably well known. Reducing opportunities for crime through better security, more surveillance and improvements to design and layout have been well documented (Department of the Environment 1992, 1993). Research shows that good management underpins crime prevention projects, whether in housing areas, schools or town centres (Home Office

Crime prevention and community safety	
A. Preventing crime:	*B. Preventing criminality:*
Reducing opportunities	Strengthening families
Designing out crime	Enhancing education/recreation
Managing out crime	Revitalising communities
Preventive policing	Creating training/employment
Preventing revictimisation	Preventing reoffending

1993b, pp.32–39). Preventive policing is an essential ingredient of many crime prevention packages. This is particularly so if officers are attached to areas for a reasonable period of time, if their work is valued by their senior officers and if they approach the prevention of crime as a problem-solving exercise (Trojanowicz and Buqueroux 1990). Such situational and enforcement measures not only make crime more difficult to commit but might be expected to place boundaries on the behaviour of young people and, in some circumstances, influence their attitudes and behaviour.

More space will be devoted to measures which aim to prevent criminality directly since they have received far less attention. The aim of the approach suggested in this chapter is to strengthen three of the main influences on children and young people, namely:

- their family
- their school
- their community

so that children and young people are better supervised, occupied more constructively, integrated within schools, assisted with training, employment and housing, included in community life and thereby diverted from anti-social behaviour and offending. The aim is to reduce the *risk factors* associated with offending such as poor parenting and school failure, and enhance *protective factors* such as good parenting and school success.[2] The whole is greater than the sum of its parts. The three elements taken together can help ensure that there is *continuity* (over

2 It is worth noting that an approach based on family, school and community-based prevention is also the core of a community drug prevention strategy (Hawkins and Catalano 1992).

time), *reinforcement* (of standards in different locations), and *inclusion* (of young people in the community).

Family-based prevention

Research conducted over half a century in a number of Western countries has consistently identified common aspects of family life that increase the risks of delinquency. These include:

- poor parental supervision
- harsh, neglectful or erratic discipline
- parental conflict
- a parent with a criminal record
- low family income
- social disadvantage.

Although it is not possible to identify any one of these as the 'cause' of delinquency, the likelihood of later criminality increases when adverse factors *cluster* together in a child's background. Those children who experience these factors at their most extreme are at greatest risk of becoming *persistent* offenders responsible for a disproportionate volume of crime.

The influence which some factors exert over children's behaviour is largely *indirect*. Low income, poor living conditions and parental conflict can be viewed as *stress factors* on parents which can reduce their ability to provide children with the care, attention and discipline necessary for successful parenting. Other factors such as poor parental supervision and harsh or inconsistent discipline have a *direct* influence on children's behaviour in the short and longer term.

This suggests that the children of parents who are warm and affectionate, but can also exert consistent, non-violent discipline are less likely to behave anti-socially or offend.

It is reasonable to assume, therefore, that programmes which improve parenting skills can play a valuable part in preventing anti-social behaviour and later criminality. Such measures are, however, unlikely to yield their full potential unless accompanied by action to alleviate at least some of the outside stresses that make it more difficult to be a 'good enough' parent.

Family/parent support programmes vary according to the intensity (and relative expense) of the service being provided. At one end of the spectrum are those whose potential clientele is every parent in the land – services provided by organisations such as *Parent Network* and *Parents as Teachers* are good examples. At the other end are organisations like *Newpin*, whose interventions are designed to help families in crisis and where children may be seriously at risk of physical or sexual abuse. In between are services provided by *family centres* and organisations like *Homestart* which tend to operate in disadvantaged neighbourhoods.

These services can be classified as follows:

> *Universal services*: available to anyone wanting to make the most of being a parent;
>
> *Neighbourhood services*: targeted on disadvantaged neighbourhoods and families under stress;
>
> *Family preservation*: targeted on individual families in crisis that have come to the attention of social services or the police.

There is some evidence for the success of these approaches. American research shows that parenting skills training can improve parenting, reduce child abuse and neglect, improve school achievement and reduce delinquency (Catalano and Hawkins 1992; Utting, Bright and Henrickson 1993, pp.34–35). Family support programmes have been shown to prevent abuse and neglect, family breakdown and out of home care, experiences often associated with delinquency (Kelly 1991; Nelson 1991).

In the UK, such services are often provided by family centres. However, isolated families living under stress may benefit from more intensive programmes that reach into their homes. Those managed by Homestart, for example, befriend families and provide assistance. One evaluation found that 86 per cent of children helped by Homestart stayed out of care (Van der Eyken 1982, 1990). In the USA, Michigan's Families First (part of the State's Social Services Department) has been able to reduce out of home care by 25 per cent. Significantly, the financial savings have been reinvested in the programme, thereby enabling it to increase its scope (Kelly 1991). The families helped by such approaches are those whose children are most at risk of being abused themselves and of behaving anti-socially and criminally as they grow up.

Of relevance in this section (although it spans home and school) is pre-school education. Good pre-school education can have many short-

and long-term benefits, including less anti-social behaviour and delinquency. It is good for both parents and children. The Perry pre-school programme in the USA strikingly demonstrates the potential benefits of high quality early childhood programmes for disadvantaged children. It shows that pre-school participation can increase the proportion of young people who at age 19 are literate, employed and enrolled in post secondary education, and can reduce the proportion who dropped out of school, had been arrested or were on welfare. It also has short- and medium-term benefits for parents and is very cost-effective. These findings still held firm at age 27 (Schweinhart and Weikart 1993).

These early childhood development services are of interest to those concerned with crime prevention because there are links between early childhood experiences and later offending and there is increasing evidence that interventions can be successful. However, they are not crime prevention programmes. Their principal objectives are to improve health, cognitive or emotional development, to reduce child abuse or to improve family functioning. Frequently they have multiple positive outcomes. They are included in this chapter because of their apparent capacity to reduce some of the risk factors associated with later offending. There is also increasing interest in the early social prevention of crime because of the limited success of remedial education and training programmes targeted at adolescent and young adult offenders.

School-based prevention

The influence of parents declines as children grow up and the process of socialisation is shared with the school. The most popular school-based approaches to reducing delinquency have been police–school liaison schemes, substance abuse prevention programmes and personal responsibility sessions on the school curriculum.

Less attention has been given to strategies which improve the management, ethos and climate of schools so that they are better able to meet the needs of those students who bring with them problems that interfere with their capacity to learn. Until recently, it was widely thought that schools could do little about students who fail or behave disruptively or truant and that these problems were largely due to the individual student and his/her family background. Research now suggests that schools can exercise significant influence over these outcomes (Graham 1988, 1990, 1995). Even when the catchment area and home background of students are taken into account, researchers have found significant differences between schools in terms of the proportion of their students who behave anti-socially and offend. Some schools in high crime areas have low delinquency rates, while others in low crime areas have high rates. This suggests that schools are able to exert an *independent* effect on student behaviour both within and outside the school.

Schools which are able to offer students a sense of achievement regardless of ability and are able to motivate and integrate them are likely to reduce the incidence of negative outcomes such as school failure and delinquency. Similarly, schools which are likely to have high rates of delinquency among pupils are those which, inadvertently or otherwise, segregate pupils rigidly according to academic ability, concentrate on academic success at the expense of practical and social skills, categorise pupils as deviants, inadequates and failures and refer responsibility for the behaviour and welfare of their pupils to outside agencies and institutions. Schools which permanently exclude their most difficult pupils, or ignore those who persistently fail to attend school, may themselves be contributing to the promotion of delinquency.

'School effectiveness' research generally, in both the UK and US, suggests that schools can have a substantial effect on student performance and thereby exercise some influence on the likelihood of young people failing school and drifting into delinquency. For example, one study found that the same child would get a CSE grade 3 in English in one school and an O level grade B in another. The differences between schools are not as great as the differences between the homes of their pupils and effective schools are not going to compensate for the enormous differences between individual pupils in terms of ability and motivation. However, the 'school effect' appears to be substantial enough to 'ratchet' up the level of educational achievement in a school and make a significant difference in the life chances of children. For some, this will increase their motivation to succeed and lead *directly* to reduced disruption, truancy and school failure and, *indirectly*, to less delinquency. The authors argue that if all schools were improved only within the current range of performance of urban comprehensive schools, this would be enough to transform the standards of secondary education (Smith and Tomlinson 1989, p.301).

There are limits, however, to what individual schools can do. The best-known study in this area also found an association between 'academic balance' and delinquency. Delinquency rates and attendance were *lower* in schools which had a relatively high concentration of pupils in the upper ability bands at intake and *higher* in those with a low proportion of low ability pupils although there were no significant differences in *behaviour in school* (Rutter 1978). It seems that schools with a high proportion of less able pupils can influence pupil behaviour in school by good management more than they can attendance and delinquency outside school. Thus, there are limits to what individual schools can do to inhibit delinquency because the academic balance of the intake is to a great extent beyond the control of the school. In addition, there can be substantial difficulties in implementing school change strategies; it appears that the leadership quality of the principal is one of the most important factors determining success.

Effective schools will, by definition, maximise the educational progress of those most at risk of school failure. In addition to a positive ethos, consistent management and sensitive pastoral care, they may also wish to give particular emphasis to preventing truancy, stimulating parental interest, making the school a community resource, encouraging peer education initiatives, preventing bullying and broadening the curriculum.

One of the few programmes that has been documented is the Yale New Haven School Development Program which seeks to improve the way schools are managed. The program model consists of a school planning and management team, a parent participation programme, a mental health team, and an academic programme.

It has had a remarkable success. In 1969, the students in the first targeted school in inner city New Haven were 18–19 months behind grade level in reading and mathematics, and there were 'serious behavior and attendance problems'. Since 1976 that school has been among the top five schools in the city in attendance and 'has not had a serious behaviour problem in a decade' (Smith and Tomlinson 1989). By 1979, students were approximately at grade level in reading and mathematics.

Staff attendance is among the best in the city and staff turnover is among the lowest. Parent participation has been responsible and enthusiastic. Attendance at school events remarkably improved. In general, the results of this project are extremely encouraging. In addition to improvements to the educational performance of the children, the programme has been able to demonstrate durability: it has now been working for 20 years; and generalisability: it has been successfully replicated in at least one other school board in another geographical area (Comer 1980).

One of the many schools in the UK that has demonstrated its effectiveness is Ruffwood School in Knowsley, Merseyside, where levels of social deprivation and crime are high and expectations of young people low. Its head teacher set out to raise expectations of his pupils both by themselves and others. The school's mission, 'Promoting a Culture of Achievement', has been pursued by:

- involving pupils in the design and care of the environment, thereby creating a sense of ownership which has led to peer pressure to maintain high standards
- tackling the high levels of truancy through a vigorous registration system which alerts staff to absence at a very early stage; strong support systems upon re-entry to school
- access to alternative education experiences such as Cities in Schools and Work Experience.

The introduction of 'assertive discipline'. This American model designed by Lee Canter rewards good behaviour and builds on success. It makes unacceptable behaviour entirely the responsibility of the perpetrator and successfully reduces 'pay-off'.

Community-based prevention

Research shows that children and young people who have a lot of unsupervised leisure time which they spend with their friends are at increased risk of behaving anti-socially and drifting into crime (Riley and Shaw 1985). Much petty crime and anti-social behaviour could be prevented by making available recreational, sporting and social activities supported by skilled staff able to motivate and involve young people. In addition, there is also a need for more focused work with those young people who are or who may become persistent offenders.

While there are few evaluations which prove unambiguously that youth work prevents crime, there is a good deal of anecdotal evidence for its value. Furthermore, recent research by the Princes Trust and Coopers Lybrand suggests that projects may not have to prevent many crimes by their participants in order to be cost-effective (Coopers

Lybrand 1994). Generally, there is a great deal of professional and community support for community-based youth projects.

Youth crime prevention strategies undertaken by many partnerships usually begin with an *audit* which assesses local problems by collating crime-related data and consulting the community, local agencies and young people. It is important to clarify the nature of the problems (anti-social behaviour, bullying, car crime, burglary), the age group responsible (8–14; 15–18; 19–25), and the type of responses that local adult residents, young people and agencies think will work.

These are likely to involve the following:

> *Project work with children and young people,* for example holiday activity schemes and youth initiatives in high crime neighbourhoods. These programmes can be put in place fairly quickly, are not prohibitively expensive, offer immediate and tangible evidence of progress, are an effective platform for multi-agency work, and can reduce crime problems, at least in the short term.
>
> *Longer-term approaches to young people at risk,* for example, social action youth projects, detached youth work, housing and employment initiatives and community mentoring schemes. These are relatively high-cost schemes working with a small number of young people, and require a longer-term funding commitment. They work with the young people most at risk of offending, can be better targeted, and are more likely to reduce youth crime than traditional youth work methods.

One example of this latter approach is an outreach youth work project in Runcorn set up by Cheshire County Council's Youth Service and Crime Concern to improve relationships between young people and the wider community. It enabled young people to find constructive solutions to their problems and reduced the incidence of anti-social behaviour and petty crime. It also created an opportunity for the young people to make a contribution to the community by undertaking a lighting survey which led to the repair of streetlamps and the installation of 150 new lights in the area six months later. Altogether, ten different groups/activities were developed, involving 50–60 young people.

A 1994 evaluation of the Project found that calls to the police attributable to rowdy youth on the estate declined dramatically between January 1993 and 1994 (Webb 1993).

To increase the chances of success with those most likely to offend, the Princes Trust/Coopers Lybrand report argued that projects should be intensive and challenging, long-term, educational and committed to prevention as an explicit objective. They should have achievable and measurable objectives and be strongly managed. An annual action plan with agreed output and outcome measures should be prepared and monitored.

Failure to apply this methodology is one of the reasons why youth crime prevention projects have found it difficult to demonstrate effectiveness. Another reason is that they may not be intensive or comprehensive enough. To increase the chances of success, youth crime prevention strategies should address *truancy and exclusion* by school age young people; training and *employment* development for at risk young people aged 15; *homelessness* through focusing on housing advice, mediation with parents, house sharing and young people leaving care.

The opportunities for some young people (such as those leaving care with little support) will be limited and they will be at greater risk of offending. Particular attention should be paid to such groups.

In the USA, more focused, comprehensive projects have been developed in many areas (Eisenhower Foundation 1993). The Eisenhower Foundation has identified model inner city youth empowerment programmes which aim to address the multiple problems faced by inner city youth. The essential elements of these programmes are:

- development of self esteem
- extended family type support
- education and mentoring
- peer group support and activities
- employment training
- employment creation and job placement.

In some cases, all these elements are necessary if programmes are to be successful. Their effectiveness has been measured by comparing arrest rates, anti-social behaviours and participation in school before, during and after the programme. Although there were measurement problems, small sample sizes and limited comparison groups, in some cases, the results were impressive and one project was able to impact on the wider community as well as on individual participants.

One UK example of this approach is the Dalston Youth Project in Hackney in east London. This is a new education and mentoring scheme managed by Crime Concern in partnership with Hackney Council, the police and the probation service. It works with young people aged 15–20 who are at serious risk of offending or who have already embarked on a criminal career. The project aims to help young people to turn around their lives, away from offending and towards positive goals related to education, training and employment and personal development. It draws on the approach pioneered in the UK by the 'Youth at Risk' organisation.

The project works with 25–35 young people in each programme which has three components. First, a week-long residential course helps them decide what they want to achieve. Second, an education/training component provides them with the necessary skills. Third, attachment to a volunteer adult mentor from the local community offers them the long-term support to see it through and realise their ambition. The first programme undertaken by the project is currently being evaluated.

Preventing reoffending

This chapter describes approaches which aim to prevent (a) young people offending in the first place; and (b) minor and intermediate offenders from becoming persistent offenders. For persistent offenders, carefully thought through criminal justice strategies will be necessary to divert them from a criminal career. Many other organisations specialise in this area so less space will be given to it here. In summary these strategies involve:

- diversion from initial processing by the criminal justice system through cautioning and caution plus
- diversion from custody through targeted community alternatives
- rehabilitation during custody
- reintegration after custody through sustaining home links during custody and providing substantial support on release, especially with regard to income maintenance, housing and training/job access.

Conclusion

This chapter began by noting the limitations of the criminal justice agencies in controlling youth crime and argued that government policy creates the context in which local efforts will be more or less successful. It described the four stages involved in developing a local crime prevention programme and stressed the need to analyse problems and think through solutions carefully. It commented on the difficulties of delivering crime prevention at a local level and argued that more attention needs to be given to the leadership of multi agency initiatives. The importance of evaluation was stressed. It then proposed a model which aims to prevent both crime and criminality in high crime locations. It argued that criminality might be reduced by implementing preventive measures focused on the family, school and community, three of the main influences on young people. Interventions at all three levels are necessary to ensure there is *continuity* (over time), *reinforcement* (of standards in different locations) and inclusion (of young people in their community).

There is an urgent need to develop a much clearer understanding of what type of interventions work best with different kinds of young people and to identify the conditions that need to be in place for them to have optimum effect. Much of the research evidence for the approaches advocated here is American (Bright 1992). Home-grown evidence is needed. This is not another plea for more research but rather for more practice based on the methodology outlined in the second section of this chapter. Demonstrating effectiveness is essential if there is to be a significant shift towards preventing crime rather than simply reacting to it. This is desirable for reasons of social justice as well as criminal justice.

References

Bright, J. (1992) *Crime Prevention in America: A British Perspective.* Office of International Criminal Justice, University of Illinois.

Bright, J. (1993) *Youth Crime Prevention: A Framework for Local Action.* Swindon: Crime Concern.

Clarke, R.V. (ed.) (1994) *Situational Crime Prevention – Successful Case Studies.* New York: Harrow and Heston.

Comer, J.P. (1980) *School Power: Implications of an Intervention Project.* New York: Free Press. Cited in *Better Beginnings.* Ontario Ministry for Community and Social Services. Ontario: Queen's Printers.

Coopers and Lybrand (1994) ITV Telethon/Princes' Trust Preventive Strategy for Young People in Trouble.

Department of the Environment (1992) *A Handbook of Estate Improvement,* Vol. 2. *External Areas.* London: HMSO.

Department of the Environment (1993) *Crime Prevention on Housing Estates.* London: HMSO.

Eisenhower Foundation (1993) *Investing in Children and Youth, Reconstructing our Cities.* Washington, DC: Eisenhower Foundation.

Farrington, D. (1987) Early precursors of frequent offending. In J. Wilson and G. Loury (eds) *From Children to Citizens,* Vol. III. *Family, Schools and Delinquency Prevention.* New York: Springer Verlag and Robbins.

Graham, J. (1988) *Schools, Disruptive Behaviour and Offending.* Home Office Research Study No. 96. London: HMSO.

Graham, J. (1990, 1995) *Crime Prevention Strategies in Europe and North America.* Helsinki: HEUNI.

Graham, J. and Smith, D.I. (1993) *Diversion from Offending – The Role of the Youth Service.* Swindon: Crime Concern.

Hawkins, J.D. and Catalano, R.F. (1992) *Communities that Care – Action for Drug Abuse Prevention.* San Francisco: Jossey-Bass.

Home Affairs Select Committee (1993) *Inquiry into Juvenile Crime.* London: HMSO.

Home Office (1993a) *Digest 2: Information on the Criminal Justice System in England and Wales.* London: HMSO.

Home Office (1993b) *A Practical Guide to Crime Prevention for Local Partnerships.* London: HMSO.

Home Office Research and Statistics Department (1992) *Research Findings No. 2.* London: HMSO.

Hope, T. (1993) Cited in *Security and Democracy.* Report of the Analytical College on Urban Safety. Paris: European Forum for Urban Security.

House of Commons, Canada (1993) Crime Prevention in Canada: Towards a National Strategy. Twelfth Report of the Standing Committee on Justice and the Solicitor General.

Kelly, S. (1991) 'The family.' In *Family, School, Community: Towards a Social Crime Prevention Agenda.* Swindon: Crime Concern.

Kinsey, R., Anderson, S. and Smith, C. (1993) *Cautionary Tales.* Aldershot: Avebury.

Nelson, D.W. (1991) The public policy implications of family preservation. In K. Wells and D.E. Biegel (eds) *Family Preservation Services*. Newbury Park, CA: Sage Publications.

Riley, D. and Shaw, M. (1985) *Parental Supervision and Juvenile Delinquency*. Home Office Research Study No 83. London: HMSO.

Rutter, M., Manghan, B., Martinore, P. and Ouston, J. (1978) *Fifteen Thousand Hours*. London: Open Books.

Schweinhart, L.J. and Weikart, D.P. (1993) *A Summary of Significant Benefits: The High/Scope Perry Preschool Study through Age 27*. Ypsilanti, MI: High/Scope Press.

Smith, D. and Tomlinson, S. (1989) *The School Effect* London: Policy Studies Institute.

Tilley, N. (1993) Understanding car parks, crime and CCTV: evaluation lessons from Safer Cities. Police Research Group Crime Prevention Unit Series, Paper 42. London: Home Office.

Tilley, N. and Webb, J. (1994) *Burglary Reduction: Findings from Safer Cities Schemes*. Police Research Group Crime Prevention Unit Series, Paper 52. London: Home Office.

Trojanowicz, R. and Buqueroux, B. (1990) *Community Policing*. Cincinnati: Anderson.

Utting, D., Bright, J. and Henrickson, C. (1993) *Crime and the Family – Improving Child Rearing and Preventing Delinquency*. London: Family Policy Studies Centre.

Van der Eyken, W. (1982, 1990) *Homestart: A Four Year Evaluation*. Leicester: Homestart Consultancy.

Webb, J. (1994) Unpublished evaluation. Swindon: Crime Concern.

West, D. (1982) *Delinquency: Its Roots, Careers and Prospects*. Cambridge, MA: Harvard University Press.

Wilkinson, C. (1993) Youth homelessness and hidden homelessness in Sunderland. Ford and Pennywell Housing Project, Sunderland.

Chapter 2

Social Crime Prevention

Juvenile Delinquency

Francis Bailleau

What is prevention?

In general, the main purpose of prevention policies is to prevent the commission of offences – and the young are generally the principal subject for these policies (Bailleau and Garoud 1990). However, it is very difficult to give one definition because every period produces a new 'definition' but the range of crime prevention measures is not unlimited. This is partly due to the fact that a close correlation can be established between categories of offences, their perpetrators and their victims.

Prevention policies usually entail two types of action:

- improving general social prevention within the population by adapting the operation of the various systems of social advancement (education, training, protection, etc.) and social control
- developing specialised prevention so as to provide whatever 'treatment' is best suited to an 'at risk' individual or group.

In this way it is possible to propose a concise classification of the different approaches on which the main crime prevention policies have been founded since the nineteenth century (Walgrave and De Cauter 1986):

The medically and clinically oriented approach, where delinquency is attributed to individual or micro-social factors. The solutions proposed – apart from treating actual offenders – are generally based on a concern to develop, in the light of a study of the population as a whole, the earliest possible treatment of vulnerable individuals or groups after the individual factors involved have been identified.

Exemplary punitive and dissuasive approaches, where the causes of the commission of an offence are deemed to stem from poor education or socialisation which needs to be put right. Three types of solution are generally envisaged from this perspective:

- intimidation through the application of severe penalties
- making the existence of the law and its workings more visible
- promotion of technical measures for individual or group protection in order to prevent the commission of offences: community policing, burglar-proofing of doors, installation of alarm systems, etc.

Societal approaches, which seek to explain crime by social imbalances and inequalities. Solutions can be found only through an overall improvement in social equilibrium, not through individual measures which would be doomed to fail since crime prevention, far from being a neutral mechanism, tends to exacerbate imbalances between social classes or groups which have different material and moral interests.

While the solutions adopted since the nineteenth century are all similar in kind and are mainly based on one or another of these approaches, different techniques have been used at different times. Each technique tried out has developed its own field of intervention, designated its own target population and generated its own means of action (Bailleau, Lefaucheur and Peyre 1985).

However, every period produces a 'new' solution in the sense that the choice of components, the weighing-up of each one and the order of priorities are different. The purpose and limits of techniques claiming to be preventive at a given time lie not so much in the techniques themselves as in the place occupied by the concept of prevention in the various systems of social action (Peyre 1986).

The formulation of a new crime policy is usually based on an assessment of the results of previous policies, whose failure is generally depicted as the consequence of a wrong approach to crime, its causes, the personality or environment of the offender and, in all cases, as the consequence of a lack of resources. Not until this preliminary observation has been made is it possible to devise solutions and measures considered capable of reducing a phenomenon presented as having in recent years undergone an exponential growth which the current policies have failed to stem. As a rule, therefore, the aim is to abandon the previously accepted solutions and propose 'new' ones deemed more appropriate to the problem.

This explains the breaks in continuity generated by the alternation of two usually mutually exclusive types of crime policy: one predominantly repressive and the other predominantly preventive.

A new situation and/or a new policy?

Originally linked to a traditional conception of prevention, 'new social strategies' have developed in recent years in many countries (Council of Europe 1984, 1986, 1988, 1989).

Although in the last decade the emphasis tended to be laid on seeking greater repressive efficiency for purely judicial techniques of crime treatment. The revival of interest in social techniques of crime prevention has not been accompanied by any systematic rejection of the old policies (Faugeron 1989).

A new situation?

Several reasons may be advanced to explain this new pragmatic trend in crime policies in Europe, such as:

- a substantial rise in petty and less serious delinquency despite an increase in the traditional resources made available to the police and/or the judicial system
- the proliferation of self-defence techniques and the growing importance of private protection systems, which have heightened the risks of social disintegration and encouraged the rise of extremism
- the emergence of a host of economic problems and their consequences for the social and vocational integration of young people in towns
- the crisis in traditional social work, which illustrates the social difficulties encountered in trying to manage the consequences of the economic crisis with the same techniques as during the post-war years of growth.

For these reasons, the main focus is the public's reactions in the light of the evolution of juvenile delinquency in Western Europe. The public have regularly expressed their feeling of insecurity and to make a response, many governments have developed new pragmatic approaches. In relation to this, it is important to note that it is very difficult

– or impossible? – to give an exact figure of juvenile delinquency for all countries (Junger-Tas 1994).

Each country has its own view of what exactly 'juvenile delinquency' is and moreover the justice systems are different. The relationship between children and the justice system is related to very different cultural notions and expectations of the family and the role of the state. For example, the age of criminal responsibility and penal majority differs considerably. And, as a result, a direct comparison between delinquency figures and rates has to be treated with a lot of caution.

For all these reasons and others, I will not give delinquency figures or rates to draw some straight comparisons over time between different countries in Western Europe, but I will outline the main evolution of juvenile delinquency which is similar in the majority of countries. There are eight points which can be made.

1. In all countries, the great majority of offences are less serious property offences.
2. Particularly since the 1970s, juvenile delinquency grew faster than the demographic rate and, after 1984, showed a relative decrease.
3. Juvenile delinquency takes place in the local area of the offender. The majority of offences are committed on their own area and generally, against persons who are in the same social class.
4. There is an increase in the number of offences committed with violence since the middle of the 1970s, particularly against the person. This largely involves male offenders.
5. The levels of involvement of girls are growing. Before, the rate was less than 10 per cent, today it is around 20 per cent. Delinquency by girls is largely property crime, which accounts for almost 80 per cent of all offences committed by girls.
6. For the less serious property offences, the offenders are younger.
7. In all countries, there is a disproportionate number of non-nationals in the official crime statistics.
8. In the past 20 years, Western Europe has known an increase in the number of drug problems: addiction, traffic, burglaries, etc., all offences which are closely linked.

On all of these points, all the experts agree that the problem starts when explanations are sought because the trends can be explained in a number of ways and generally, each expert adopts one or two perspectives and ignores others.

Putting these eight points in context, it is necessary to recall that Western European countries have known an important increase in social difficulties since the middle of the 1970s. Our society has become less and less cohesive, the gap between the rich and the poor has grown and there are a lot of serious internal social tensions today, particularly for juveniles.

For many young people it is more and more difficult to participate in mainstream social life actively: many know poverty, marginalisation and the exclusion linked with the problem of youth unemployment.

A new policy?

While these policies have been described as 'new', it is clear in fact that their novelty lies not so much in the actual approaches and techniques as in the way they are implemented, not so much in what practitioners are involved as in the forms of their collaboration.

These new approaches are aided by two shifts:

- the transition from crime management to security management: over and above the prevention of prohibited acts, the crime prevention policies pursued in recent years, particularly since the early 1980s, have been aimed at reducing the social tensions liable to create feelings of insecurity (Bailleau and Garioud 1989)
- the return to a broader interpretation of the concept of prevention after a period dominated by a particular and more narrowly defined form of crime prevention, that is, specialised prevention.

It is important to understand the significance of these different approaches because of what has been called 'the crisis of criminal justice' (De Celis and Hulsman 1982). The most visible expression of this crisis is the fact that an increasing number of offences cannot be dealt with by the present overloaded criminal justice system. As a result, either certain offences will escape prosecution and will not therefore be dealt with at all, or they will be dealt with partially, in an unsatisfactory manner and with uncertain results; or again a solution will be found in other ways, outside the judicial system, thus aggravating the risks of social inequality. In addition, the neglect of victims of offences and the failure of the judicial system to meet their expectations are increasingly resented.

Four principles can be used to describe the 'new' policies (Conférence européenne et nord-américaine sur la securité et la prévention de la criminalité en milieu urbain 1989):

- the legitimacy of a prevention policy which includes repression; recognition of the responsibility of local government in the pragmatic management of security
- the desirability of public participation; the need for a communication policy

On this basis, the new policies have produced a variety of responses to the feeling of insecurity. In fact they have offered a framework providing a means of overcoming the old barriers between the central and the local level, between officials and politicians, among different administrations themselves, and between citizens and those responsible for ensuring their security.

The main aim is to suggest *intermediate solutions* so as to create *alternatives* to judicial intervention and thus eliminate its inevitability. Avoiding this cumbersome, costly and often ineffective encounter comparable to using a sledge-hammer to crack a nut is also a way of combating one of the causes of recidivism, viz. stigmatisation. These new procedures thus seek to render effective the principle of *individualisation*, which is aimed at adapting solutions as fully as possible to both instigator and the victim of a social disorder.

The 'new' policies – the foundations

Experiments in the various countries show that, in the matter of prevention, strategies should not be exclusive but *complementary*. Hence the need for permanent machinery for the purposes of consultation, planning and coordination. Moreover, the need is stressed for *local knowledge* of crime patterns. Such knowledge should embrace not only the cause of crime but also its manifestations, perpetrators and victims. It should be accompanied by an inventory of locally available resources and of information on prevention techniques.

To describe, at the European level, this new form of social crime prevention, four other points will be presented.

Local level

All the experiments conducted in different European countries stress the local level as the most suitable one for, if not drawing up prevention policies, at least applying them. A neighbourhood is often suggested as the ideal geographical and social area of intervention (Lurigio and Klein 1989). The ability to operationalise prevention policies at the regional level will depend on its administrative and political situation, which also varies from one country to another. The national structure, which usually exists, plays mostly a role of stimulation, coordination, planning, financing and sometimes supervision.

Thus, most of the arrangements introduced in Western countries include a national (in some cases, an interministerial) authority:

- in France, the National Crime Prevention Council, now part of the Interministerial Delegation for Towns and Urban Social Development (DIV)
- in the Netherlands, the National Crime Coordinator, who comes under both the Ministry of Justice and the Ministry of the Interior
- in Belgium, England and Wales, the Home Office or Ministry of the Interior
- in Denmark and Norway the Ministry of Justice.

While they may be initiated by central government, almost all prevention programmes will be tailored to local requirements, and they will all be applied locally. All are based on local offices, units or committees, one of the most sophisticated examples of which is undoubtedly the municipal crime prevention councils established in France in 1983 and now to be found in nearly 700 municipalities.

Experience shows that the dynamic of local level action must be given political, financial and technical support by the central level, that is, the state.

One of the most appropriate forms of support seems to involve the contractualisation of relations between the state and local authorities. The concept of a contract presupposes the determination of aims, in some cases the introduction of supervisory procedures and in all cases a reciprocal commitment seen as the guarantee of local autonomy.

Partnership

These prevention policies are all aimed at breaking down the traditional barriers between the different practitioners in this field, whether they be traditional practitioners with a possibly reoriented role, or newcomers. Partnership involves representatives of administrations as varied as those responsible for housing and town planning, justice, education, culture, vocational training, sport and recreation, health and internal affairs, as well as members of private bodies such as tenants' associations, sports clubs and bodies concerned with drugs control, the elderly and neighbourhood activities, not forgetting charitable bodies and heads of firms, etc.

Partnership is aimed at the pooling of information as well as resources (in the broad, not merely financial, sense) with a view to a common approach towards prevention.

Such co-operation may be given an institutional form, as in France with its municipal crime prevention councils, or in the Netherlands, which has committees consisting of police officers, local representatives and prosecutors. It may be less organised in other countries. Some prefer these informal arrangements because of their greater flexibility and innovation, while others consider they may give rise to civil rights violations.

Overall approach

Local coordination may take a variety of forms but this may be necessary because of the increasing prevalence of an overall approach to the problems concerned. This is true whether the policies followed have the declared aim of prevention in which case they are usually a response to a specific and/or local outbreak of social disorder or to a particular type of behaviour whether they are geared to a more general aim of social well-being to which they contribute in the same way as policies relating to cultural development, the rehabilitation of housing, the social integration of minorities, the vocational training and integration of marginalised populations.

Experience has shown that it is not enough to make it physically impossible for offences to be committed – which is the aim of situational and, more broadly, of community prevention – but that it is also necessary to tackle the social, economic and cultural factors which induce potential offenders to commit them.

The arrangements introduced in France since 1981 are a good example of such an approach. It was as a result of eruptions of violence in the suburbs of several large French cities that various policies were adopted with the explicit or implicit aim of preventing crime.

In response to these social disorders, action was taken on two fronts. Concurrently, an in-depth study was carried out by two working groups consisting of mayors and various specialists.

The first group, whose concluding report 'Face à la délinquance, prévention, répression, solidarité' was signed by Gilbert Bonnemaison (1982), a mayor, focused on a number of key ideas:

- consultation and desegregation at grassroots level
- the complementary character of prevention, penalisation and solidarity
- a contribution by all citizens to the achievement of security; and the practical nature of the measures recommended.

At the same time, Hubert Dubedout, also a mayor, was asked to make a study in low-cost housing areas of 'the implementation of genuine local plans for economic and social development dealing comprehensively with the problems of housing, transport, education, vocational training, employment and social action' with a view to combating 'the grave threats of social disintegration and the break-up of the local community', which are a hotbed of crime.

Both the Bonnemaison and the Dubedout groups referred to violence in the suburbs. As part of a contractual policy between the state and local authorities, plans for the renovation of housing and the provision of social support were negotiated for more than 150 neighbourhoods.

In 1988 the complementarity between these two groups led to their fusion within the National Council for Towns and Social and Urban Development, whose executive body is the Interministerial Delegation for Towns. In the field, the municipal crime prevention councils and the work of the French Office for the Social Development of Neighbourhoods are frequently supplemented by local projects aimed at the social and vocational integration of young people as well as the designation of priority education areas (special educational support in disadvantaged neighbourhoods) and by the 'Suburbs '89' unit (a group of architects seeking to change the image of suburban housing estates).

Community participation

An overall approach does not necessarily mean 'mass action'. It is true that a number of prevention programmes are planned at a central decision-making level, with a view to being applied throughout a country or the greater part thereof; but their implementation is nevertheless highly individualised and often limited to a particular area. They involve the concept of neighbourhood, the unit often chosen for community policing, urban renewal, socio-educational and cultural provision. It is also at the neighbourhood level that community participation develops spontaneously or is most frequently sought.

Community participation takes many forms, ranging from voluntary co-operation in police activities (exchanges of information) to the introduction of neighbourhood watch groups (Husain 1988), via the teaching of new practices to local inhabitants, such as avoiding certain places and protecting one's own home.

This involvement of the public in the protection of their neighbourhood and in their own security is based on information which increasingly makes use of the mass media.

'Security is everyone's business.' While this principle is supported by all those responsible for crime prevention policies, there are, however, some notable differences between countries, which suggests that a cultural explanation should be sought for this state of affairs.

- Britons, Canadians and, even more so, Americans are in favour not only of 'passive defence' (avoidance strategies, individual protection and situational prevention) but also of participation in 'offensive' actions designed to ensure their own security and that of their neighbours (co-operation with the police, creation of deterrent areas) (Newman 1972)
- The Scandinavians are strong supporters of situational prevention. Spaniards, Italians and the French are somewhat hesitant about a high degree of personal involvement.

Community crime prevention schemes first arose in the mid-1970s. They are now almost as varied as they are numerous. However,

> The fundamental philosophy of community crime prevention is embodied in the notion that the most effective means of combating crime must involve residents in proactive interventions and participatory projects aimed at reducing or precluding the opportu-

nity for crime to occur in their neighbourhoods. (Lurigio and Rosenbaum 1988, p.46)

Most schemes are based on the fact that criminals operate in a context which includes the police, citizens and the physical environment (Kelling 1988). These three components are, as it were, what determines the opportunities for committing an offence. The aim of the schemes is therefore to vary the components and, above all, make them interact in order to reduce the opportunities. This approach is especially prevalent in the Scandinavian countries: 'The focus is not on eradicating the causes of crime, but affecting the opportunity for its commission. "Opportunity makes the thief" is a common phrase in criminological circles' (Friday 1988). Thus local inhabitants are asked, in co-operation with the security authorities, to organise their social and physical environment in such a way as not to encourage the commission of offences or, if an offence is committed, to enable the offenders to be immediately detected.

Community prevention programmes also call on the public to contribute towards neighbourhood surveillance. Inhabitants of a neighbourhood are also advised to mark their possessions indelibly. They may likewise organise their own patrols of their buildings or neighbourhoods. They are provided with means of giving the alarm (whistles, telephones). Groups of inhabitants, some of whom may be security professionals, can go round inspecting homes to detect weak points in the protection system and suggest improvements.

The development of new social strategies for avoiding the production of criminal behaviour is generally based on recognition of the fact that the criminal justice system alone cannot ensure the maintenance of the social order.

This justification for bypassing the traditional modes of social regulation is inadequate unless accompanied by an assessment of the results of such strategies and, more broadly, of their consequences. But, any assessment can only be relative, as any strategy is highly dependent on the social, economic and political context in which it is deployed, the persons responsible for implementing it, the resources available to them and the population aimed at. Accordingly, the choice of a particular scheme is, put rather prosaically, dependent on the estimated costs rather than the expected benefits.

There will always remain the problem of a balance between freedoms and security. But, in the absence of any precise legal framework, it is important in the development of preventive strategies that three rules be respected in order to protect individual freedoms:

- the right of all citizens to come and go without constraint
- the right of victims of offences to receive just reparation, both material and moral
- the right of offenders to be given a just penalty which will not hinder their social rehabilitation.

Crime prevention has both to recognise and be limited by acknowledgement of these three principles.

References

Bailleau, F. and Garioud, G. (1989) Violence et sécurité: l'impossible partage. In *L'état de la France et de ses habitants*. Paris: Éditions la Découverte.

Bailleau, F. and Garioud, G. (1990) Les stratégies sociales visant à éviter la production de comportements criminalisables. XIX° conférence de recherches criminologiques. Strasbourg: Conseil de l'Europe.

Bailleau, F., Lefaucheur, N. and Peyre, V. (1985) *Lectures sociologiques du travail social*. Paris: Éditions Ouvrières.

Bonnemaison, G. (1982) *Prévention, repression, solidarité*. Rapport remis au I Ministre, Paris, décembre.

Conférence européenne et nord-americaine sur la sécurité et la prévention de la criminalité en milieu urbain (1989a) Montréal, octobre.

Conférence européenne et nord-américaine sur la sécurité et la prévention de la criminalité en milieu urbain (1989b) 'Pour des villes plus sûres.' Déclaration finale, Montréal, 10–13 octobre 1989.

Council of Europe (1984) La participation du public à la politique criminelle. Rapport du comité européen pour les problèmes criminels, Strasbourg.

Council of Europe (1986) La violence et l'insécurité urbaines: le rôle des politiques locales. Conférence permanente des pouvoirs locaux et régionaux de l'Europe, Strasbourg, 10 octobre.

Council of Europe (1987) Conférence sur la prévention de l'insécurité urbaine. Déclaration finale. Conférence permanente des pouvoirs locaux et réligionaux de l'Europe, Barcelone, 17–20 novembre.

Council of Europe (1988) Organisation de la prévention de la criminalité, Strasbourg.

Council of Europe (1989) Sur la réduction de l'insécurité urbaine. Résolution de la Conférence permanente des pouvoirs locaux et régionaux d'Europe, 24° session, Strasbourg, 7–8 mars.

De Celis, J.B. and Hulsman, L. (1982) *Peines Perdues: le Système Pénal en Question*. Paris: Éditions le Centurion.

Faugeron, C. (1989) Crime prevention policy: current state and prospect. European Colloquium on Crime and Public Policy in Europe, Max Plank Institute, September.

Friday, P.C. (1988) The Scandinavian efforts to balance societal response to offenses and offenders: crime prevention and social control. *International Journal of Comparative and Applied Criminal Justice* 12, 1, Spring.

Husain, S. (1988) *Neighbourhood Watch in England and Wales: A Locational Analysis*. Crime Prevention Unit, Paper 12. London: Home Office.

Junger-Tas, J. (1994) *Delinquent Behavior among Young People in the Western World.'* Ministry of Justice, Amsterdam.

Kelling, G. (1988) Police and communities: the quiet revolution. *Perspectives on Policing*. National Institute of Justice, Havard University, No.1, June.

Lurigio, A.J. and Klein, L. (1989) Controlling crime in the community: citizen-based efforts and initiatives. *Crime and Delinquency* 35, 3, July.

Lurigio, A.J. and Rosenbaum, D.P. (1988) Evaluation research in community crime prevention. In A.J. Lurigio amd D.P. Rosenbaum *Community Crime Prevention*. Newbury Park, CA: Sage publications.

Newman, O. (1972) *Defensible Space, Crime Prevention through Urban Design*. New York: Collier Books.

Peyre, V. (1986) Conférence introductive aux actes des cinquièmes journées internationales. In V. Peyre (ed) *Délinquance des jeunes*. Volume 2. Vaucresson: Éditions du CRIV.

Walgrave, L. and De Cauter, F. (1986) Une tentative de clarification de la notion de prévention. *Les annales de Vaucresson*, no. 24, Vaucresson.

Chapter 3

Children's Hearings and Children in Trouble

Janice McGhee, Lorraine Waterhouse and Bill Whyte

Background to the hearings system

The Children's Hearings System in Scotland was established under the Social Work (Scotland) Act 1968 and came into operation on 15 April 1971. This innovation in dealing with children in trouble was a direct result of the deliberations of the Kilbrandon Committee, who sought to find solutions to the rise in the rate of juvenile delinquency in post-war Scotland. Evidence gathered at the time indicated the triviality of most of the offences dealt with in the juvenile courts where 37 per cent of disposals in 1962 were either subject to absolute discharge or admonition. It was further found that in 95 per cent of cases there were no disputes as to the facts alleged and only 5 per cent were guilty pleas (Cooper 1983).

The committee found that the legal distinction between juvenile offenders and children in need of care and protection was not a meaningful distinction when the underlying circumstances and needs of the children were examined. This has remained the central philosophy of the system where 'needs' rather than 'deeds' are the basis for decision making and intervention.

Kilbrandon saw the desirability of a national machinery to deal with children where services should be coordinated for children in difficulty. He envisaged a new 'social education department' located within education authorities to be responsible for providing services to deprived and delinquent children. This would include both field and residential services and would exercise the duties which probation officers (and subsequently social services departments) carried out in England in regard to child offenders.

There were concerns, however, from social work professionals both about their role in the proposed new 'social education departments' and the lack of emphasis on social measures to resolve child and family difficulties. The lack of flexibility within Scottish education at that time, with its emphasis on parental responsibility for the child's behaviour, was seen as thwarting the emphasis within social work on the need to assess all the factors (social, environmental, and individual) which influence a child's development. Education alone was seen as providing too narrow a focus for the wide-ranging, complex needs of children in trouble.

The outcome of debate and lobbying by social work associations and academics led to the creation of the social work departments as we know them today. In Scotland there is no separate probation service; social work services carry out the duties associated with probation in England and Wales, these duties having been integrated into their remit alongside responsibility for child care. This was a surprising development considering the punitive attitudes towards adult offenders in Scotland.

This enlightened system has also attracted criticisms both nationally and internationally which have focused on the tension between justice and welfare (Adler 1985). Since its inception the Children's Hearings System has given rise to debate about the balance to be struck between justice, the rights of children, their parents and the welfare of children. This debate was brought into public focus by the Orkney (Scottish Office 1992a) and Fife (Scottish Office 1992b) inquiries, and the recent case of O v Rae 1992 SCLR 318 has drawn further attention to this argument whereby the children's hearing was able to make decisions using information which could have founded a condition of referral but had not been tested before a sheriff.

This tension is particularly stark in child protection cases where the interests of parents may be in conflict with the child. Since 1985 the chairperson of a hearing and also the sheriff have been able to appoint a safeguarder in situations where there is a conflict between the interests of a child and his/her parents. Most recent Scottish Office figures (Scottish Office 1993) indicate that safeguarders were appointed in 1.6 per cent of cases in 9646 disposals in 1988, compared with 3.6 per cent of 8449 disposals in 1993. Safeguarders are more likely to be appointed for children attending a hearing referred on non-offence grounds (5.9% of 4484 cases in 1993) than children referred on offence grounds (0.7%

of 3106 cases in 1993). Nonetheless, there has been continuing disquiet about the ability of lay panels to address the complex nature of these cases and to arbitrate between the potentially conflicting interests and rights.

Despite the controversy over this system there has been a dearth of social research into the operation of the system, decision making at all levels, and child care outcomes. The major empirical study was that by Martin, Fox and Murray which reported in 1981 on information relating to the period 1978–79. Other major writing about the system has largely been about the philosophical (Adler 1985) or legal functioning of the system (Kearney 1987). Other research has focused on limited aspects of the system (see for example, Bruce and Spencer (1976) on the initial implementation of the system; Lockyer (1988) on the relationship between social work recommendations to hearings and the decisions taken; and Finlayson (1993) on Reporters' accountability).

In view of this, the Scottish Office has commissioned a study of the operation of the Children's Hearings System in two parts. The first concerns the processes of decision making within the Hearings System; the second is a national study of the characteristics and outcomes for children who are referred to the Reporter and followed up over three years. These studies should highlight the rationale for decisions taken and provide a picture of the social backgrounds and experiences of children within the Hearings System. It is also expected that any progression to the adult criminal justice system will be examined.

As Kilbrandon intended, the Children's Hearings System separated the functions of looking at the needs of children from establishing guilt. The courts were only to be involved where the facts were disputed, for appeals and dealing with more serious offences. Children under 16 years of age can only be prosecuted in the criminal courts at the instructions of the Lord Advocate. It remains an early intervention system for those children who would benefit from compulsory measures of care and protection. It is not a court but a tribunal serviced by lay people drawn from the community of the child with knowledge of children and family life. Each local authority has a Children's Panel Advisory Committee which has the responsibility for recruiting and training lay panel members and ensuring members carry out their duties satisfactorily. Many more people apply than are accepted which may suggest popular support for and understanding of the system.

Each region currently has a department of the Reporter to the Children's Panel and whilst the Reporter is employed by the local authority s/he is independent and can only be removed by the Secretary of State for Scotland. The Reporter is the 'lynch-pin' (Thomson 1991) of the system, s/he receives all referrals and decides if there is sufficient evidence to establish a condition of referral and whether a child may be in need of compulsory measures of care which include protection, control, guidance and treatment. The Reporter's options include the decision to take no further action, to refer to the social work department for voluntary measures of care or to arrange a children's hearing.

Reporters come from a range of disciplinary backgrounds although law, social work and to a lesser extent education dominate. The separation of departments has led to differing local practices both in decision making and response to referrals. This has given rise to concern and with the Local Government (Scotland) Act 1994 a new centralised service will be introduced with the advent of local government reform in Scotland in April 1996. There will be a Principal Reporter and a Children's Hearings Administration responsible for a national service. This may ensure the development of more standardised procedures and decision making.

The process of the hearing

A children's hearing involves three lay members of the panel (one of whom chairs the meeting), the parents or guardians of a child, the child in the majority of cases, representatives from the social work department, and the Reporter who provides legal advice to the hearing but does not take part in the proceedings. There is provision for parent(s) and/or the child to bring a representative, who may be a friend or a legal adviser, although legal aid is not available at this stage. The chair has the responsibility for the formal aspects of the proceedings and puts the grounds of referral to the child and his/her family. If the child and/or parent/guardian do not accept the grounds, or the child is too young, or is unable to understand the grounds, then the proceedings stop. The chair asks the Reporter to refer the matter to the sheriff and a formal court hearing will be heard in chambers to establish if the conditions for the grounds are met. Legal aid is available at this stage. If the child has been offended against the abuser does not have to be named, unlike in a criminal prosecution, and proceedings do not have to await the outcome of any criminal prosecution.

If the grounds are established the case is remitted back to the children's hearing for disposal; if the grounds are not upheld the case is discharged. For those cases which proceed to a hearing where a supervision requirement is made there is a system of review to establish progress and ensure that compulsory measures of care continue to be required. Review is annual unless requested earlier by the child and/or parent(s) or social work department.

The social work department provides reports and is responsible for the care and supervision of the child. A recent European Court of Human Rights decision has criticised the UK for refusing to giving parents the right to see any written reports provided by professionals. While it is certainly accepted social work practice to allow family members the opportunity to read reports this remains discretionary. The Children's (Scotland) Bill 1994 included proposals to allow increased access to professional reports.

Statistical trends

In 1993 24,304 children were referred to the Reporters' Departments of which 15,622 were boys and the remainder girls. This reflects a steady increase in the number of girls referred under 16 years. The pattern for boys continues to decrease although the overall rate per 1000 of the population for boys is higher than the comparable figure for 1972 (the first year of the operation of the Children's Hearings System). The increase in the number of referrals for girls is likely to be associated with the overall increase in care and protection grounds while for boys the decrease is associated with a reduction in offence grounds. In 1993 there was a 7 per cent decrease in the number of offence grounds from 1992.

The official statistics highlight the changing pattern of referrals to the children's hearings system. Martin, Fox and Murray (1981), in a study completed soon after the inception of the hearings system, drew attention to the predominance of offence referrals. They found of 678 cases 73 per cent of first grounds of referral were for offences, while only 5 per cent were related to parental neglect or an offence committed against a child. This trend has changed dramatically in the intervening 15 years. Most recent Scottish Office statistics (Scottish Office 1994) show for the first time the rate of children referred to reporters on non-offence grounds exceeded those of offence grounds with a non-offence rate of 13.5 in 1993 compared with an offence rate of 11.9 in 1993. The grounds of referral to a Children's Hearing are set out in s.32(2) Social Work (Scotland) Act 1968.

Gender differences in referral

The last ten years have seen a steady increase in the rate of non-offence grounds from 5.0 in 1983 to 13.5 in 1993. The most common ground of referral for both girls and boys was ground (d) where the child was a victim of neglect, assault or ill-treatment. However there was a clear gender difference, as of all referrals on this ground 40 per cent related to girls compared to 33 per cent for boys. This contrasts with ground (c), lack of parental care, where boys and girls were equally affected in 1993, constituting about one-fifth of all referrals.

It is also interesting to note that referrals for ground (f), non-attendance at school, increased by 9 per cent in 1993 for girls but only 4 per cent for boys. This has worrying implications for the educational attainments of children, especially girls, who may already be disadvantaged within educational settings. It has also been found that children in public care suffer from disruptions in their educational experience which may account for their subsequently poor performance on standardised examinations (Milham *et al.* 1986).

Loss of schooling in children who are already facing adversity appears to have further negative consequences for later life chances. Rutter and Quinton (1988), looking at outcomes for young people raised in institutions, have shown the importance of positive school experiences in mediating adverse adult outcomes where home circumstances were characterised by poor relationships. Schooling is of central importance to children who come from already difficult backgrounds whilst for children from ordinary backgrounds good experiences at school make little difference to how they fare. This would seem to support Kilbrandon's early formulation of an emphasis on 'social education' for children.

This is particularly relevant for girls where research has shown that choice of partner is likely to reflect their own circumstances of disadvantage and to further limit their horizons (Rutter and Quinton 1988). Girls who come from backgrounds of family discord and experience institutional care are more likely to select deviant partners perhaps as a well-intentioned but misguided escape from discordant relationships at home. Positive educational experience can in effect widen the choice of partner, research having shown that a supportive marital relationship is a protective factor against stressful experiences (Brown and Harris 1978) and may support reasonable child rearing practice (Rutter and Quinton 1988).

This serves to illustrate the double jeopardy which girls in our society are currently facing, where not only are they more likely to be the victim of an offence – Dobash, Carnie and Waterhouse (1993) found girls were significantly over-represented as victims of sexual offences – but they also face an increased likelihood of missing out on educational experiences which may be vital to their future well-being.

Martin, Fox and Murray (1981) found the peak age for referral to a Reporter for both boys and girls was 12–15-year-olds with 10,699 out of a total of 13,566 boys and 2791 out of a total of 3742 girls referred in that year (p.38, table 3.5). This finding is further reflected in the 1993 statistics which show a similar gradual rise in referrals to the Reporter for both boys and girls for the ages 12–15.

There has been a fluctuating but slightly decreasing rate of referral on offence grounds from 13.2 in 1983, through 14.6 in 1987 to 11.9 in 1993, 15 years remaining the peak age for both boys and girls for alleged offending. Compared to children aged 8–11 years the rate of referral for both boys and girls is similar for non-offence grounds but boys are over-represented for offence related grounds with 1507 boys compared to 173 girls referred to Reporters for alleged offences in 1993. The comparable figures for boys and girls on non-offence grounds are 1499 for boys and 1245 for girls.

It is not clear whether the increased offence referrals for boys in this group reflect a real increase in offending behaviour or are an artefact of legal definitions with similar behaviours being redefined as offending but previously categorised under care and protection. The age of criminal responsibility in Scotland is 8 years. It remains unclear how children who enter the Hearings System under offence grounds fare in the longer term both in relation to subsequent criminality and later social functioning compared to those who enter under non-offence grounds. Nor is it clear what proportion of children move between these two categories throughout their childhood. How many children who enter the Hearings System on care and protection grounds at an early age subsequently re-enter at a later stage on offence-related grounds?

Although Kilbrandon strove to place the emphasis on needs rather than deeds the continuing differentiation between offenders and non-offenders has always remained and is reflected in the different standards of legal proof. Children who are offended against require grounds to be established on the civil standard of proof (the balance of probability) while for offenders the criminal standard (beyond reasonable doubt) has been retained.

Children who offend in Scotland

Children and young people in Scotland represent about 11 per cent of the population yet commit between 20 and 40 per cent of reported crime. The peak age of offending remains mid to late teens reducing to a relatively small percentage by age 20 (Scottish Office 1990, 1991, 1993). Less serious offences typically, vandalism, theft from cars are common at age 15; more serious offences, particularly involving violence, between 17 and 19. It is therefore not unusual for young people to get into trouble, but the majority do not come to the formal attention of the authorities beyond a transient involvement. Most stop offending of their own accord without any need for formal intervention.

Anderson and Kinsey (1993) compared self-reports of offending behaviour in both disadvantaged and advantaged areas of a Scottish city. They found over two-thirds (69%) of all the young people reported having committed at least one offence during the previous nine months, with a third (27%) of these reporting a moderately serious offence. No significant social class differences were found, suggesting infrequent, non-serious offending is the norm rather than the exception.

Social hardship may not be a good predictor of those who offend although research shows it is a good predictor of those more likely to be processed through formal systems (Farrington 1993). Closeness of parental supervision and levels of parental expectation of behaviour regarding offending were more important predictors of offending behaviour. This would suggest the use of informal processes and diversion from prosecution are the most appropriate way of dealing with the majority of children who get into trouble. In 1993 around two-thirds of those reported for offending were not brought to a hearing although the long-term outcome for these children is not known (Scottish Office 1994).

Longitudinal and 'meta-analytic' studies (for example Lipsey 1990) are beginning to confirm factors which strengthen Kilbrandon's emphasis on 'social education' as an effective response to children and young people who offend. Gendreau and Ross (1987), in examining over 300 studies carried out between 1973 and 1987, concluded that almost all successful programmes had one common characteristic – the utilisation of cognitive-behavioural techniques. These techniques focus on developing problem-solving skills, critical reasoning and an understanding of the thoughts and feeling of other people.

Persistent offenders

There is growing concern about young people who persistently offend with a belief that these youngsters tend to be specialist criminals, for example, making a living out of stealing cars. Hagel and Newburn (1994), in their research, identified 531 10–16-year-olds in two areas in England who had allegedly committed at least three offences in 1992. The most common were road traffic offences, theft from shops and car theft. Violent and/or sexual crimes were unusual and drug related offences were apparently rare. Few were employed, or in further education or training, and 50 per cent were already known to social services. Patterns of familial disruption characterised by alcohol and/or drug misuse as well as criminality within the family were reported.

The researchers further analysed the sample by applying definitions of persistent offender, as follows: the top 10 per cent charged or thought to have committed most offences in the area; those known or alleged to have committed 10 or more offences in a single three month period; those meeting the Home Office criteria for secure training orders (that is, those who have committed three or more serious offences, one of which must have been committed while on supervision). Eight children from the original sample met the definition of serious offender, only three of whom were in the 12–14 age group.

There was little evidence of criminal specialism: offences varied greatly; patterns of offending were not continuous but tended to involve bursts of activity over short periods then cessation. Adverse personal and social circumstances were the common factors among the children rather than the nature of their offences. All reported high levels of offending and drug use; all had been in care and were described as having chaotic family backgrounds: their schooling was characterised by truancy and exclusion. None offended entirely on their own but usually with others they had met in care or elsewhere in the local area. This research provides support for Kilbrandon's contention that defining children in criminal terms alone is unhelpful when the differences between children who offend and those in need of care and protection are far outweighed by their similarities.

Some critics suggest that the Hearings System does not succeed with persistent young offenders (Pease and Barlow 1989). This may be argued either because social work intervention is said not to systematically address offending behaviour, or because the young people are invariably discharged from supervision at 16 years when offending behaviour tends to increase (Save the Children 1992). The Criminal Procedure (Scotland) Act 1975 makes provision for adult courts to remit all offenders under 18 to the Hearings System for advice or disposal. This seldom occurs, Murray (1983) contending this may be partly related to the Lord Advocate's instructions (1982) for Procurators Fiscal to bring 16- and 17-year-olds to court unless special circumstances indicate they should be dealt with by the Hearings. In 1992 Scottish courts remitted only 40 cases, out of 36,089 involving males aged 16–20, to the Children's Hearings (Scottish Office 1993, p.19). There is some evidence to indicate that this age group is disadvantaged by untimely discharge from the Hearings System.

Kennedy and McIvor (1992), examining all 16–17-year-olds appearing in one sheriff court, found that 53 per cent had previous appearances in the Hearing System, with all but one having been on supervision, the majority having been discharged at age 16. These young people were found to have similar characteristics to the persistent offenders described by Hagel and Newburn (1994): they had been referred frequently to the reporter; had a history of prior social work involvement with periods in care or under supervision; and family and personal problems. Nearly three-quarters (70%) were unemployed and 40 per cent had a history of truancy. They were more likely to have experienced a range of custodial and social work disposals than young people who had not had prior involvement in the Hearings System.

Sources of referral

Law enforcement agencies continue to dominate as key sources of referral to Reporters. Martin, Fox and Murray (1981) found that nearly 80 per cent of all referrals came from law enforcement agencies (that is, police (65%), courts (1%) and Procurators Fiscal (13%)). This pattern has remained remarkably consistent from 1983 to 1993 at around 78 per cent (Scottish Office 1994). Similarly, Martin *et al.* (1981) found that alleged offence grounds constituted 73 per cent of all referrals to Reporters while in 1993 Scottish Office statistics showed this figure to have had a small but steady decline from 74 per cent in 1989 to 67 per cent in 1993.

Social work and education departments contributed 19 per cent of all referrals in Martin *et al.* (1981) study and have remained consistently at this level throughout the past 10 years. This pattern has been found in other child care research. For example, Packman (1986) and Vernon and Fruin (1986) found the influence of law enforcement agencies was central in the identification of children who may be in need of social work intervention. Their influence in the decision whether to admit to public care was critical, but if we look at the Hearings System Martin *et al.* (1981) found the opposite effect in that a referral from the school or social work department was much more likely to result in a subsequent referral to a children's hearing than if the source of referral was one of the law enforcement agencies.

There are no comparable statistics available for 1993 but Harvey (1994), in an unpublished report, noted that a higher proportion of non-offence referrals proceed to hearings. She found in 1991 42 per cent of cases referred to a hearing were on non-offence grounds compared with 31 per cent on offence grounds. This may give some support to the pattern found by Martin *et al.* (1981) remaining the same, as police are the most common source of offence referrals.

Parental referral to the Reporter has remained at exactly the same level of 1 per cent found by Martin *et al.* (1981) throughout the past 10 years (Scottish Office 1993). This is perhaps surprising when the original idea was to encourage families to come forward for help to a universally available social service comparable to health and education.

Kilbrandon had predicted that in the main the offences committed by children would not be of a serious nature. Martin *et al.* (1981)

examined the seriousness of alleged offences and found that of the 514 offences allegedly committed theft (40%) and housebreaking (19%) were the most common. Violence only accounted for 3 per cent and public order and property damage was (17%) (table 5.3, p.67). Current statistics do not routinely report the seriousness of offences alleged and therefore direct comparison is not possible. However in cases involving children under 16 referred to the court in 1992, most resulted in admonition, discharge, supervision or fine, which would suggest that they were not considered serious offenders (Scottish Office 1993, p.19).

Variations in Reporter's practice

The Children's Hearings System includes a diversionary element demonstrated in the discretion afforded to Reporters in their decision making. Martin *et al.* (1981) highlight a range of influences on this decision making including personal conviction, group norms and departmental practice. Variation in decision making was reduced by regionalisation but still exists both between and within districts in Regions.

There is recognition that decision making should reflect local concerns and interest. Scottish Office statistics reflect this continuing variation with, for example, Strathclyde referring 37 per cent of all referrals to children's hearings in 1993 compared to Central with only 17 per cent. However, this disguises a general reduction in the percentage of referrals which went to hearings between 1990 and 1993 (Scottish Office 1994). Shetland is an outstanding example of this trend, with 29 per cent of referrals going to hearings in 1990 rising to 36 per cent in 1991 and dropping to 12 per cent in 1993. Most other Regions have had a small but steady decline and this may reflect a greater emphasis on the diversionary aspects of the system which may be further amplified with the institution of a National Reporters Administration. The number of children referred to a hearing on non-offence grounds has remained consistently higher than referrals on offence grounds throughout.

Decisions of hearings

The most frequent disposal by hearings is a non-residential supervision requirement accounting for 85 per cent of all disposals by hearings in

1993 (Scottish Office 1994). This pattern of disposal varies by grounds of referral but not apparently gender. Of the children who were not currently under supervision when referred to a hearing 55 per cent of boys and 54 per cent of girls referred on offence grounds were placed on supervision while for children referred on non-offence grounds the comparable figures are much larger for both boys and girls with 80 per cent and 79 per cent respectively. Over all age groups the use of supervision is increasing although this is most marked for the youngest children. Since 1983 the rate per 1000 of children under 5 years subject to a supervision requirement has consistently increased up until 1991, since when there has been a small decrease. Even taking into account this recent decrease the rate in 1993 is still nearly twice that of 1983.

Discussion

The original philosophy of Kilbrandon to focus on 'needs not deeds' attempted to emphasise the similarity between children in need of care and protection and those who primarily came to the attention of the authorities because of their offending. The individual welfare of both groups of children was seen as the common focus for decision making and intervention. While on one level both these groups appear to face similar adverse social and family circumstances the apparent lack of direct attention towards offending behaviour may have served to undermine confidence in the system to deal with persistent offenders.

Similar concern is reflected in other jurisdictions which have moved towards different solutions for children who offend compared to those in need of care. This is exemplified in England and Wales where there are plans to introduce secure training units for persistent offenders. This reflects a growing punitive approach towards juveniles in trouble with an emphasis on mandatory sentencing of increasing length and a preference for adult models, which risk dissolving the important distinction between adult and juvenile justice. If this trend were to develop in Scotland then the Children's Hearings System will either have to alter their approach to juveniles in trouble or face a declining role in decisions about their future.

Nearly 25 years later the gap Kilbrandon tried to close between the needs of children in trouble with the law and children in need of care is beginning to open. As Cleland (1995) suggests, this change in outlook is reflected both in the United Kingdom and abroad and is likely to pose a serious challenge to the philosophy which lies behind the Children's Hearings System. She argues increased public pressure to make children accountable for wrongdoing, plus a growing concentration on the needs of victims, have contributed to the public focus shifting from the welfare of the child to offending behaviour and its consequences.

As outlined earlier Kilbrandon found the majority of offences committed by children were not serious in nature. Although there are no recent comparable statistics for children under 16 years, young people 16 years and over referred to the adult court have tended to receive minor sentences for what are therefore likely to be minor offences. Kilbrandon may have underestimated the problems posed to the system by children who persistently offend, but Hagel and Newburn's (1994) research affirms the adversity of their personal and social backgrounds in comparison to other children who offend.

Policy appears to be shifting from a concern with the social and personal needs of juvenile offenders to the frequency and nature of their offences. These are not necessarily mutually exclusive but a balance needs to be struck between addressing offending behaviour and responding to the needs of children in trouble.

These arguments are reflected in child protection policy and practice within the United Kingdom, where an increased emphasis is given to investigation and surveillance and less on the welfare of the child through provision of universally available child care resources. There is a similar danger that focusing on offending behaviour alone will hinder the development of wider social and educational resources necessary for all children especially those who are disadvantaged. Hallett (1993), comparing European and UK practices in relation to child protection, stresses the need to strike a balance between the paramountcy of the welfare of the child and the notion of justice within the wider community. This struggle is also played out in relation to children who offend. The law and social work practice have attempted to balance these competing claims against a growing background of public policy which seeks to isolate the young offender for the protection of the community.

The Children (Scotland) Act addresses some of these concerns although it does not increase the powers of the hearing to deal with young offenders. However it appears sheriffs may be able to substitute their own judgement in appeals from hearings. It remains to be seen how this new power will be utilised but it may suggest a possible shift to the adult justice system for contested cases on both offence and non-offence grounds.

Conclusion

The Children's Hearings System was seen to be an enlightened and progressive way of dealing with the welfare of children in trouble. Empirical evidence to support or refute its effectiveness is still very thin on the ground despite the conceptual battles between the System's protagonists and critics over the emphasis on justice or welfare. The lack of research into the System may prove to have been a major policy error creating a vacuum for specific groups to project their own vested interests. The lack of baseline information against which to measure the performance of the Hearings System leaves it vulnerable to political influence and public pressure. The principles which Kilbrandon fought for at a time when juvenile crime was rising seem to these writers to be as relevant today. The current desire to remove young offenders from child care decision making to a justice model risks stepping back into failed past experiments rather than addressing the social and family conditions which may contribute towards offending behaviour.

References

Adler, R. (1985) *Taking Juvenile Justice Seriously*. Edinburgh: Scottish Academic Press.

Anderson, L., Kinsey, R. and Smith, C. (1993) *Cautionary Tales, A Study of Young People and Crime in Edinburgh*. Edinburgh: Criminal Research Unit, Scottish Office.

Brown, G.W. and Harris, T.O. (1978) *Social Origins of Depression: A Study of Psychiatric Disorder in Women*. London: Tavistock Publications, New York: Free Press.

Bruce, N. and Spencer, J. (1976) *Face to Face with Families. A Report on the Children's Panels in Scotland*. Loanhead: Macdonald Publishers.

Cleland, A. (1995) Legal solutions for children: comparing Scots Law with other jurisdictions. *Scottish Affairs 10*, Winter, 6–24.

Cooper, J. (1983) *The Creation of the British Personal Social Services 1962–74*. London: Heinemann Education Books.

Dobash, R., Carnie, J. and Waterhouse, L. (1993) Child sexual abusers: recognition and response. In L. Waterhouse (ed.) *Child Abuse and Child Abusers: Protection and Prevention*. London: Jessica Kingsley Publishers.

Farrington, D. (1993) Juvenile delinquency. In J. Coleman (ed.) *The School Years*. London: Routledge.

Farrington, D. and Hawkins, J. (1991) Predicting participation, early onset, and later persistence in officially recorded offending. *Criminal Behaviour and Mental Health* 1, 1–33.

Finlayson, A. (1993) *Reporters to Children's Panels. Their Role, Function and Accountability*. Edinburgh: Social Work Services Group, Scottish Office. HMSO.

Gendreau, P. and Ross, R. (1987) Revivification or rehabilitation: evidence from the 1980s. *Justice Quarterly* 4, 349–407.

Hagel, A. and Newburn, T. (1994) *The Persistent Offender*. London: Policy Studies Institute.

Hallet, C. (1993) Child protection in Europe: convergence or divergence? *Adoption and Fostering* 17, 4, 27–32.

Harvey, J. (1994) The Children's Hearings system in Scotland: key issues for research. Unpublished manuscript. Edinburgh: Scottish Office.

Kearney, B. (1987) *Children's Hearings and the Sheriff Court*. Edinburgh: Butterworths/The Law Society of Scotland.

Kennedy, R. and McIvor, G. (1992) Young offenders in the Children's Hearing and criminal justice systems: a comparative analysis. Unpublished report for Tayside Regional Council.

Kilbrandon, L. (1964) *Children and Young Persons, Scotland*. Cm 2306. Edinburgh: Scottish Home and Health Department.

Lipsey, W. (1990) Juvenile delinquency treatment: a meta-analytic enquiry into the viability of effects. In T. Cook *et al.* (eds) *Meta-Analysis for Explanation*. New York: Sage.

Lockyer, A. (1988) *Study of Children's Hearings Disposals in Relation to Resources. Children's Panel Chairman's Group*. Edinburgh: Macdonald Lindsay.

Martin, F.M., Fox, S.J. and Murray, K. (1981) *Children Out of Court*. Edinburgh: Scottish Academic Press.

Millham, S., Bulock, R., Hosie, K. and Haak, M. (1986) *Children Lost in Care. The Family Contact of Children in Care*. Aldershot: Gower.

Murray, K. (1983) Children's Hearings. In J. English and F. Martin (eds) *Social Services in Scotland*. Edinburgh: Scottish Academic Press.

Packman, J., Randall, J. and Jacques, N. (1986) *Who Needs Care? Social Work Decisions about Children*. Oxford: Basil Blackwell.

Pease, J. and Barlow, G. (1989) *Contradictions Inherent in the Children's Hearing System*. Edinburgh: Scottish Child and Family Alliance (now Children in Scotland).

Rutter, M. and Quinton, D. (1988) *Parenting Breakdown. The Making and Breaking of Intergenerational Links*. Aldershot: Avebury.

Save the Children (1992) *16 and 17 Year Olds at the Interface between the Children's Hearings System and the Criminal Justice System*. Glasgow: Save the Children.

Scottish Office (1992a) *The Report of the Inquiry into the Removal of Children from Orkney in February 1991*. Edinburgh: HMSO.

Scottish Office (1992b) *Inquiry into Child Care Policies in Fife*. Edinburgh: HMSO.

Scottish Office (1990,1991,1993) *Statistical Bulletins: Criminal Proceedings in Scottish Courts*. Edinburgh: Government Statistical Service.

Scottish Office (1994) *Statistical Bulletin, Social Work Series. Referrrals of Children to Reporters and Children's Hearings 1993*. Edinburgh: Government Statistical Service.

Thomson, J.M. (1991) *Family Law in Scotland*. 2nd ed. Edinburgh: Butterworths/The Law Society of Scotland.

Vernon, J. and Fruin, D. (1986) *In Care: A Study of Social Work Decision Making*. London: National Children's Bureau.

Chapter 4

The Organisation and Functioning of Juvenile Justice in England and Wales

John Graham

Introduction

This chapter describes the juvenile justice system of England and Wales. Following a brief description of the principal developments in juvenile justice since the beginning of the twentieth century, it describes the main changes in juvenile justice brought about by the most recent changes in the law. This is followed by a description of the current overall response to juvenile offending, including pre-trail arrangements and a detailed description of the wide range of sentencing options available to the youth court.

Brief history

The first juvenile courts were established by the 1908 Children Act. With the exception of murder, they dealt with all offences committed by young persons aged between 7 and 15, unless the offences were committed with an adult. Following the introduction of this Act, only children aged 14 and over could be sentenced to imprisonment, and for 14- and 15-year-olds, imprisonment could only be enacted if the court issued an 'unruly' certificate.

In 1933, the first Children and Young Persons Act introduced the concept of welfare provision into the juvenile justice system, placing a duty on magistrates to have regard to the welfare of the child in making an appropriate disposal. The 1933 Act, which extended the jurisdiction of the juvenile court to 16 year olds, introduced approved schools, which provided juvenile offenders with education and training, and remand homes, which kept remanded juveniles apart from adult prisoners.

After the war, corporal punishment was abolished by the 1948 Criminal Justice Act, which also marked the beginning of a trend towards increasing restrictions on the use of imprisonment for juvenile offenders. The age below which an offender could be sentenced to imprisonment (with the exception of certain grave crimes) was raised to 15 and detention centres were introduced for short periods of custody (usually three months, but exceptionally six months). The first detention centre opened four years later in 1952. The 1948 Act also introduced remand centres and attendance centres, the main purpose of the latter being to punish by depriving the offender of his/her leisure time. In the same year, the Children Act set up local authority children's departments which, among other things, ended the placement of neglected children alongside offenders in approved schools.

The 1961 Criminal Justice Act removed from juvenile courts the power to sentence young offenders to prison for more than six months (with a few exceptions). The Act also reduced the maximum period of borstal training from three years to two years and lowered the minimum age from 16 to 15. Section 53 of the Children and Young Persons Act 1933, which provided for the detention of young people for certain grave crimes, was expanded for those aged 14 and above, to all offences for which an adult sentence of 14 years or more might be imposed. Two years later, the Children and Young Persons Act 1963 raised the age of criminal responsibility from 8 to 10.

The trend towards a welfare-oriented system culminated with the passing of the Children and Young Persons Act in 1969, which shifted the emphasis away from matters of justice and legal rights and towards the welfare of the child and his/her immediate needs. The 1969 Act also shifted the balance of power away from magistrates and towards the local authority, which became responsible for implementing some of the disposals of the juvenile court, such as care orders and intermediate treatment. Approved schools and remand homes were amalgamated into community homes, which were run by local authorities, and committing an offence became one of the grounds on which care proceedings could be brought.

In practice, the Act was never fully implemented, and by the end of the 1970s the welfare approach was increasingly being questioned. Arguments prevailed for a return to a 'just deserts' model, for proportionality in sentencing (that the penalty should be proportional to the seriousness of the crime), for determinate penalties and for greater protection of the legal rights of juveniles (and their parents). Legislation passed during the 1980s went some way to achieving these objectives.

The 1982 Criminal Justice Act abolished indeterminate sentences (borstal training was replaced by youth custody with a maximum period of 12 months), shortened sentences of imprisonment in a detention centre from a minimum of three and a maximum of six months to 21 days and four months respectively, and introduced criteria for restricting the use of custody. The 1982 Act also allowed new requirements to be attached to supervision orders and the following year the Department of Health issued a Circular announcing the allocation of funds for diverting young offenders from custody through intensive intermediate treatment programmes and encouraging local authorities to set up inter-agency committees for dealing with young offenders. This, it has been suggested, constituted a first step towards a more integrated system of juvenile justice (Allen 1991).

Up to the end of the 1980s, the history of juvenile justice was characterised by contrasting views on the causes of (and hence remedies for) offending. Legislation and criminal justice policy and practice swung towards and then away from a welfare approach to juvenile offenders, at times emphasising the needs of the child, at others the importance of punishment. The 1988 Criminal Justice Act strengthened the criteria for imposing a custodial sentence and replaced detention centres and youth custody with a single custodial sentence known as 'detention in a young offender institution' for those aged 15 and above. A year later, the Children Act 1989 finally removed all civil (care) proceedings from the juvenile court, leaving it to deal exclusively with criminal matters. Throughout the 1980s the recognition that certain categories of offenders are best dealt with outside the formal court system was underlined by the increasing use of the police caution. A series of Home Office Circulars encouraged the use of cautioning and culminated in 1990 with the introduction of National Standards (revised in 1994). The 1980s also witnessed a decline in the use of custodial measures for juvenile offenders.

The 1991 Criminal Justice Act

At the beginning of the 1990s the 1991 Criminal Justice Act (implemented 1 October 1992), which currently provides the general legal framework for the adjudication of young offenders, reflected a move away from a welfare approach and towards a 'just deserts' approach. It followed the 1989 Children Act, which reinforced the welfare principle in non-criminal proceedings affecting children, and abolished the criminal care order. Responsibility for dealing with young offenders also shifted again, this time away from the criminal justice system as a whole and towards the community. It confirmed in legislation the move towards diverting young offenders from court and custody by bringing 17-year-olds within the jurisdiction of a new youth (as opposed to juvenile) court (see also Home Office Circular 30/1992). This change brought the sentencing of 17-year-olds into line with the age of majority and with sentencing practice in other Western European countries (Gibson *et al.* 1994). It remains to be seen to what extent the inclusion of 17-year-olds in the newly named youth court will alter the welfare ethos of juvenile justice proceedings.

As part of a trend towards gradually removing those aged under 14 from the formal jurisdiction of the courts (Gibson *et al.* 1994), the 1991 Act explicitly distinguished between 'children', who are aged 10 to 13, and 'young persons', who are aged 14 to 17 inclusive. This trend was temporarily halted following a Court of Appeal judgement in 1994 (Court of Appeal in C (a minor) v Director of Public Prosecutions (1994)), which ruled that children aged 10 to 13 were *doli incapax*, which means that they are fully capable of criminal intent. This decision has, however, recently been overturned by the House of Lords on the grounds that such matters are properly a matter for Parliament to decide. On the basis that their offending rates were found to be almost identical, 16- and 17-year-olds were identified by the 1991 Act as 'near adults' and sentenced on the basis of their maturity rather than their age. However, 17-year-olds continued to be dealt with as adults for remand and other pre-trial purposes.

The 1991 Act contains a twin track approach to offenders, distinctions being drawn between a minority of violent, dangerous and persistent offenders, for whom custody is likely to be the right option, and a majority of mostly petty property offenders, for whom community based sentences are considered more appropriate. The main changes introduced by the Act which apply specifically to juvenile offenders were that remands in adult custody for 15- and 16-year-old boys were to be phased out, the maximum term of detention in a Young Offenders Institution was reduced to 12 months, parents were made more accountable for the offences of their children and a range of new community penalties were made available to the courts. Additionally, the 1991 Act required probation and social services departments to prepare local 'action plans' for dealing with young offenders, especially 16- and 17-year-olds. These 'action plans' set out local arrangements for servicing the youth court with pre-sentence reports, carrying out orders made by the courts and conducting post-custody supervision.

Recent developments

In 1993, a new Criminal Justice Act reversed a number of key provisions in the 1991 Act, including the introduction of the unit fine system and the restrictions imposed on sentences in considering previous convictions and sentences when assessing the seriousness of an offence for arriving at an appropriate sentence. Offences committed while on bail became an aggravating factor in sentencing decisions and the maximum penalty for causing death by dangerous driving, or by careless driving while under the influence of drink or drugs, was increased from 5 years to 10 years. This was followed in 1994 by the Criminal Justice and Public Order Act, which is the most recent legislation affecting juvenile offenders.

The 1994 Criminal Justice and Public Order Act represents a partial reversal of the diversionary trend which characterised the 1980s. It introduces a range of new measures which essentially extend the courts' remand and sentencing powers to younger offenders. Thus a new custodial sentence for 12–14-year-old persistent offenders – the secure training order – has been introduced and the provisions of section 53 of the Children and Young Persons Act 1969 on detention for grave offences (that is, those which for an adult carry a maximum sentence of 14 years imprisonment) has been extended to 10–13-year-olds and, in the case of indecent assault on a woman, to 10–15-year-olds. The 1994 Act also increases the maximum length of detention in a Young Offenders Institution from 12 to 24 months for 15–17-year-olds, allows courts to remand 12–14-year-olds as well as 15- and 16-year-olds to secure accommodation and provides courts with new powers to bind over parents to ensure compliance by their child with a community sentence. Further details of some of the provisions in this Act, and in particular those pertaining to the new secure training order, are dealt with further below (see also Wilkinson 1995).

Current arrangements for dealing with young offenders

The earliest age at which a child can be brought to court in criminal proceedings is 10 years. This is known as 'the age of criminal responsibility'. A child below the age of 10 cannot be found guilty of a criminal offence. The judicial arrangements for dealing with young offenders (those aged 10 to 17) can be divided into four main sections: (1) cautioning; (2) prosecution; (3) remand arrangements and (4) sentencing, which includes a description of the sentences currently available for young offenders under the age of 18.

Cautioning

When dealing with a young offender, the police have considerable discretion in deciding how to respond. They may decide, in the most trivial cases, that an informal warning is sufficient, either given on the spot or at the police station. In either case no further action will be taken. Informal warnings are not recorded and cannot be cited in court. If an informal warning is not considered appropriate, the police may decide to caution the young person. The purpose of a formal caution is defined as being:

- to deal quickly and simply with less serious offenders
- to divert them from the criminal court
- to reduce the chances of reoffending.

Before a caution is given:

> there must be evidence of the offender's guilt sufficient to give a realistic prospect of conviction; the offender must admit the offence; the offender, and in the case of a juvenile under 17 his parent or guardian, must understand the significance of a caution and give informed consent.

The police are also required to consider whether a caution is in the public interest, taking into account the nature of the offence and whether a caution is likely to be effective.

Some cautions are administered within a few hours of the commission of the offence; in other cases, police officers may decide that further information about the young person is required, necessitating a visit to the young person's home or an approach to other agencies. Inter-agency panels, which include representatives of the probation service, education service and social services, have been set up in many areas and may be consulted in difficult cases. Home Office Circular 18/1994, which sets out guidance on the cautioning of offenders and includes revised National Standards, now rules out, save in the most exceptional circumstances, the use of cautioning for serious offences and severely discourages repeat cautioning.

In deciding on whether to caution, additional services or assistance may be offered to the young person or to his or her family. Under the Children Act 1989, local authorities are under a duty to take reasonable steps to reduce the need for criminal proceedings to be brought against children in their area. In discharging this duty some local authorities have established a range of support services, including facilities such as mediation and reparation schemes. The Government is considering the formalisation of 'cautioning plus' schemes, but there are no immediate plans to introduce a legislative framework for governing cautioning, as recommended by the Royal Commission on Criminal Justice (1993) and endorsed by the Home Affairs Select Committee report on Juvenile Offenders (1993).

Prosecution

If a decision is taken not to caution but to pursue a prosecution, the case is then referred to the Crown Prosecution Service (CPS), who will decide whether there is sufficient evidence to secure a conviction and whether it is in the public interest to proceed with the prosecution. If not, the CPS will discontinue proceedings, sometimes referring the case back to the police with a recommendation for a caution. Since the introduction of the Crown Prosecution Service in 1986, the proportion of cases discontinued has increased considerably.

Remand arrangements

Once a decision has been taken to prosecute an offender, he/she will be bailed to appear in court. The Bail Act 1976 applies to juveniles in the same way that it applies to adults, and while there is a general presumption in favour of bail for all defendants, this is particularly emphasised in the case of juveniles. Under the 1976 Act, the presumption is that defendants will be granted bail, unless the court is satisfied that there are substantial grounds for believing that the defendant, if released on bail, would:

- fail to surrender to custody, or

- commit an offence while on bail, or
- interfere with witnesses or otherwise obstruct the course of justice.

Additionally, defendants may be refused bail if the court is satisfied that they should be kept in custody (or local authority accommodation) for their own protection or, if they are under 17, for their own welfare. The 1994 Criminal Justice and Public Order Act has tightened some of the conditions under which bail may be granted. A detailed guide to the principles and procedures relating to bail can be found in Cavadino and Gibson (1993), and Home Office Circular 69/1994 offers those who make, or are in some way concerned with bail decisions, guidance and advice on how to improve bail information and thus risk assessment.

In many areas bail information schemes are available although these currently only apply to those aged 17 and over. These provide detailed and verified information about the defendant and his domestic circumstances which helps courts decide whether the general presumption in favour of bail should or should not be overruled. In 1993, the Home Affairs Select Committee on Juvenile Offenders (1993) recommended that the use of bail information schemes by the courts when dealing with offenders under the age of 17 should become standard practice. New national standards on bail information schemes were subsequently produced and these came into effect in March 1995. In some parts of the country community programmes, provided either by the voluntary sector or by local authorities, are available for work with defendants who might be at risk of being refused bail in the absence of some kind of support and/or supervision.

If bail is refused, a juvenile offender may be remanded either to local authority accommodation or to prison.

Remands to local authority accommodation

Defendants under 17 who are refused bail are normally remanded to local authority accommodation, usually in the area in which the young person resides or where the offence was committed. The local authority has broad discretion over where the juvenile is placed, although following the implementation of the Criminal Justice Act 1991, courts now have a power to impose conditions on the defendant and a power to impose requirements upon the local authority (see below). A wide range of alternative forms of residential provision is available for juveniles remanded to local authority accommodation, depending on the circumstances of the young person concerned. The placement possibilities include: a community home (sometimes in secure conditions); remand fostering; supported lodgings; placement with relatives or placement in his/her normal home.

Accommodation in a community home

A high proportion of young people remanded to local authority accommodation are accommodated in community homes. These provide an alternative to the family home for those who have difficulties with their families. Under certain circumstances juveniles held on remand in community homes may, on application by the local authority to a court, be held in secure accommodation. Only those with a high risk of absconding, or those charged or convicted of a serious offence (violent, sexual or punishable in the case of an adult with 14 years imprisonment or more) are likely to be held in secure accommodation. (Although the 1991 Act provides for 15- and 16-year-olds, but not 17-year-olds, to be remanded in secure accommodation rather than prison custody, this will only be fully realised once sufficient provision has been provided). The 1994 Criminal Justice and Public Order Act extended the age range of children on whom courts are empowered to impose a 'security' requirement from 15 and upwards to 12 and upwards. These provisions will only be implemented once sufficient secure accommodation is available.

Remand fostering

As an alternative to accommodation in a community home, a young person may be placed with remand foster parents, who will usually have been specially recruited and trained for the purpose. Fostering can be more effective than a community home placement, allowing for more individual attention, supervision and support. The number of remand foster schemes is small, but growing.

Supported lodgings

Where a local authority decides that a young person is not in great need of supervision or support, it may place him/her in private lodgings. The host family is not usually expected to fulfil a parental role, but to offer a degree of support.

Placement with relatives

This placement may be used when factors associated with the juvenile's own home suggest that a removal from this environment would be desirable and where relatives are willing and able to offer support and supervision.

When a defendant is remanded to local authority accommodation, the court may impose other special conditions, such as requiring the defendant to remain indoors between certain hours, to refrain from attending a particular place or meeting particular individuals, or to report to a police station. The court can also impose requirements upon the local authority, such as stipulating that the defendant shall not be placed (that is, accommodated) with a named person. For example, the court may take the view that the home circumstances of the defendant provide insufficient support or supervision and may decide, therefore, to require the local authority not to allow him/her to return to live at home.

Remands to prisons

Since the mid-1970s it has been the aim of successive governments to phase out the remanding of juveniles to penal establishments and between 1977 and 1981 the powers of the court to remand juveniles in custody were progressively restricted. Fourteen-year-old girls were excluded from the procedure in 1977, 15- and 16-year-old girls in 1979 and 14-year-old boys in 1981. Since then custodial remands for juveniles have been available only for 15- and 16-year-old boys and the numbers remanded in prison fell substantially during the 1980s, only to begin rising again in the last couple of years.

Remands in prison are subject to similar criteria as for placement in secure accommodation, with the added criterion of protecting the public from serious harm from the young person. Before remanding a young person to prison the court is required to consult a local authority social worker or a probation officer. No young person may be remanded to prison without having been given the opportunity of applying for legal aid. The Criminal Justice Act 1991 contains the power to replace prison remands with remands to local authority secure accommodation for 15- and 16-year-olds of either sex and it is expected that prison remands for all 15- and 16-year-olds will be phased out over the next few years.

Sentencing

The powers of the courts to sentence offenders under 18 are governed by a number of key principles. First, sentences must relate primarily to the seriousness of the current offence, and in the case of sexual and violent offences, the need to protect the public from serious harm from the offender. Second, courts remain subject to the general principle set out in the Children and Young Persons Act 1933 that, in dealing with a child or young person, whether as an offender or otherwise, they shall have regard to the welfare of the child or young person. Third, in the case of defendants under the age of 15, parents are expected to attend court and to pay any fines or compensation. Courts are required to bind parents over to take proper care of and exercise proper control of their child where this is desirable and in the interests of preventing the commission by him (or her) of further offences. The 1994 Criminal Justice and Public Order Act extends these powers by allowing courts to include in any bind-over a requirement that the parent or guardian ensures that a child complies with the requirements of a community sentence.

A fourth principle relates to the special status of 16- and 17-year-olds who are regarded as being in a transitional stage between childhood and adulthood and for whom it is believed that a flexible approach to sentencing is desirable. The full range of community sentences, both those previously available for juveniles and those currently available for adults, can be imposed and courts have powers to involve parents rather than the duty to do so which applies in respect of younger offenders. In determining how to use these powers, courts are required to take account of a range of factors relating to the offender's stage of development and maturity.

Most proceedings in respect of people under 18 are brought in specially constituted magistrates' courts known as youth courts. The procedure in youth courts, which is adversarial in nature, is simpler and less formal than in adult magistrates' courts. Members of the public are not admitted to sittings of youth courts but the press may attend and report the proceedings. However, such reports must not identify any young people involved unless the court itself has allowed identification so as to prevent injustice to a juvenile or facilitate a serious offender's apprehension. The magistrates who sit in youth courts are chosen from a special panel. The court must be made up of not more than three magistrates, among whom there must normally be at least one man and at least one woman. Most magistrates are unpaid, or 'lay' members of the public who rely on justices' clerks for advice on matters of law. In some large cities, stipendiary magistrates are appointed; they are full time, salaried professionals with legal qualifications who adjudicate alone.

Before imposing custody (except in indictable only offences or where the sentence is prescribed in law), or certain more demanding community sentences (for example, community service orders and combination orders or a supervision order with requirements), the 1991 Criminal Justice Act provided that the court should consider a pre-sentence report (PSR). The report, which should be submitted by a probation officer or a social worker, attempts to reach an opinion on the most suitable sentence for the offender based on information relating to the offender and the circumstances of the offence, including mitigating factors. National Standards for PSRs were published in 1992 and new standards were published in March 1995. The intention of the report is not to make firm recommendations to the court as to an appropriate sentence, but to draw the court's attention to various considerations in the event of passing a community or custodial sentence. The 1994 Criminal Justice and Public Order Act provides the courts with the discretion to dispense with the requirement to obtain a PSR before sentence where it is satisfied that it can properly sentence without one and if it has considered an existing PSR on the offender concerned. (If more than one such report exists, the most recent one must be considered.) This is an extension to summary cases and cases triable either way of the discretion available under the 1991 Criminal Justice Act in indictable only cases. It has been suggested that, in practice, courts would be unlikely (Wilkinson 1995) or unwise (Faulkner 1995) to dispense with PSRs for juvenile offenders.

Under certain circumstances a child or young person will be tried in the Crown Court rather than the Youth Court. These circumstances include: those charged with homicide; those charged with an offence for which a person aged 21 or over could be sentenced to at least 14 years imprisonment; those charged with the offence of indecent assault on a woman; and those charged jointly with a person aged 18 or older (who may also be committed to an adult magistrates court).

Sentences available for young people aged under 18

A range of sentences is available for juvenile offenders aged 10 to 18. These can be broadly divided into four kinds:

- discharges
- financial penalties
- community sentences
- custodial sentences.

Discharges

As they can with adults, courts can make an order discharging a child or young person. An absolute discharge is used where the offender is convicted but no further action is needed. Under a conditional discharge, there is no immediate further action, but the offender remains liable to punishment for the offence if he is convicted of a further offence within a period specified by the court but not exceeding three years.

Financial penalties

Fines, compensation orders and orders to pay the costs of the prosecution may be made against young people under 18 in much the same way as against adults, but there are important differences. Since 1933 courts have been able to require the parent or guardian to pay, rather than the young offender. Where the offender is under 16, courts are under a duty to order the parent or guardian to pay, unless the parent or guardian cannot be found, or where it would be unreasonable to do so. Where the offender is 16 or 17 the court's duty to order the parent to pay the fine is replaced by a power to do so.

Compensation orders are available for offenders of any age. They may be imposed with any other sentence or as the only sentence. The maximum is £5000 in youth courts. The means of the person actually paying the sum will be relevant in determining the level of any compensation awarded.

Where children and young people under 16 are convicted of an offence, courts have a duty to bind over their parents to take proper care and exercise proper control over them, if the court believes that to do so would help prevent the commission of further offences by the juvenile. Courts have a power to bind over the parents of 16- and 17-year-olds.

A bind over means that the parents may be ordered to pay a sum of money specified by the court (up to £1000) if they fail to look after their children properly. If they refuse unreasonably to be bound over, they can be fined up to £1000.

Community sentences

Under the Criminal Justice Act 1991, the attendance centre order, supervision order (with and without requirements), probation order, community service order, combination order and curfew order are all known as community sentences. To coincide with the implementation of the 1991 Act, the government published National Standards in 1992 to strengthen the supervision of offenders in the community by setting a clear framework of expectations and requirements for the supervision and enforcement of community penalties. Community sentences fall into two categories: those available for the full youth court age range and those only available for 16- and 17-year-olds.

Attendance centre orders

The aims of the attendance centre order are to impose a loss of leisure and to encourage young offenders, in a disciplined environment, to make more constructive use of their leisure time. Ten- to 15-year-olds can receive orders of 12 to 24 hours in a junior attendance centre, whereas 16- and 17-year-olds can receive orders of up to 36 hours, which can be in either a junior or a senior (up to the age of 21) centre. (Where the offender is aged under 14 the court has discretion to impose an order of less than 12 hours). Centres are usually open for two to three hours every other Saturday. The expectation is that, with regular attendance, offenders should be able to complete their orders within six months.

Supervision orders

A child or young person aged 10 and under 18 may be placed under the supervision of a social worker or a probation officer for a period of up to three years. A supervision order is similar to a probation order for adults, although there are some differences. It is not necessary to have the consent of the juvenile to the making of the order, although this consent is required where additional requirements are included (see below).

The three principal objectives of the supervisor are:

- to encourage and assist the child or young person in his/her development towards a responsible and law abiding life, thereby promoting the welfare of the offender
- to protect the public from harm from the offender
- to secure the rehabilitation of the offender and prevent him/her from committing further offences.

Supervision orders with requirements

A wide range of requirements can be added to a supervision order by the court or, under delegated authority, by the supervisor. The juvenile may be required, for example, to live at a particular place for a specified period; attend at a specified place at specified times or take part in various forms of activities. The kind of activities usually undertaken include: discussions with young people on ways of avoiding further offending; reintroduction to school or education; tackling any problems related to health, drink or drugs; resolving relationship difficulties within the juvenile's family; and, in appropriate circumstances, offering help with housing and employment opportunities.

Where the court does not delegate authority to the supervisor but itself decides what requirements to attach to the supervision order, it may choose two further types of requirement, in addition to those already specified above. It may require the juvenile to remain at a specified place or places (one of which must be his home) for specified periods between 6 pm and 6 am unless he is accompanied by his parent, guardian, the supervisor or by some person specified in the order. Alternatively, it may require the juvenile to refrain from specified activities for specified periods during the duration of the supervision order.

Three further requirements which a court may attach to supervision orders are: a requirement for mental treatment; a requirement to attend school and a requirement not to reside with certain named people.

Probation order

Probation orders place juvenile offenders aged 16 or 17 years under the supervision of a probation officer for a period of between six months and three years. Offenders must consent to a probation order and, as with supervision orders, a wide variety of conditions may be imposed, including a requirement to attend a probation centre or to undergo treatment for drug and alcohol dependency. Reparation and mediation between an offender and a victim can also form part of a probation (or supervision) order.

Community service orders

Community service orders are also available for juvenile offenders aged 16 and 17, but only for offences punishable with imprisonment and, like for probation orders, only where the offender consents to such an order. Their purpose is to engage young offenders in work of benefit to the local community, such as clearing litter, for between 40 and 240 hours. Before making the order the court must be satisfied that the offender is a suitable person to perform community service and that such work can be made available locally. A community service order must be completed within 12 months of the making of the order. Juvenile offenders who are in breach of a community service order can be sentenced to custody. Community service has been available for 17-year-olds since its introduction in 1973, and for 16-year-olds since 1983.

Combination orders

Combination orders are available for juvenile offenders aged 16 and 17. They combine elements of both probation and community service and like both, they are available only for offences punishable with imprisonment. In principle, the full range of additional requirements available for probation orders is available also for combination orders. They are aimed at offenders who the courts believe should make some reparation to the community through community service and who also need probation supervision. Orders are for between 12 months and 3 years probation supervision and can include between 40 and 100 hours community service.

Curfew orders

16- and 17-year-olds can also receive curfew orders, requiring them to remain at a specific place for specific periods of time. The Criminal Justice Act 1991 made provision for an order to include requirements for securing the electronic monitoring of the offender's whereabouts during the curfew periods. Pilot projects which will assess the effectiveness of electronic monitoring of curfew orders were due to begin in June 1995.

Custodial sentences

There are two kinds of custodial sentences currently available for young people under 18: detention in a Young Offender Institution and long-term detention under Section 53 of the Children and Young Person's Act 1933.

Detention in a Young Offender Institution (YOI)

Detention in a YOI is available for young people aged 15 and above. The minimum sentence is two months and the maximum two years. Criteria for restricting the use of custody for young offenders have been in operation since the introduction of the Criminal Justice Act 1982. The reason for seeking to restrict the use of custodial sentences is the recognition of the status of young offenders as children and the view that an adult length of sentence would be inappropriate and potentially counter-productive for most offences committed by children.

A court cannot pass a custodial sentence unless it is of the opinion:

1. that the offence or the combination of the offence and one other offence associated with it is so serious that only such a sentence can be justified for the offence, or
2. where the offence is a violent or a sexual offence, that only such a sentence would be adequate to protect the public from serious harm from him.

Detention under Section 53

Detention under Section 53 is a sentence only available following conviction in the Crown Court for children and young people aged 10 and above who commit 'grave crimes', (that is, offences of murder, manslaughter and other offences which, in the case of an adult, carry a maximum sentence of at least 14 years (for example, rape, robbery, arson, domestic burglary and indecent assault on a woman). Those convicted of murder receive an indeterminate sentence similar to life imprisonment in the case of an adult. Offenders sentenced under Section 53 for other grave crimes receive determinate sentences of up to the statutory maximum for the offence.

Young people detained under Section 53 are held either in Young Offender Institutions or secure child care establishments. Offenders under the age of 16 are generally placed in the child care system, whilst those over the age of 16 are generally allocated to YOIs unless reports indicate that they are immature or particularly in need of the kind of care and attention they would receive in a child care establishment. The number of juveniles sentenced under Section 53 in 1993 was 339, which represents a threefold increase on the figure for 1991.

All young offenders sentenced to a YOI or under Section 53 must have at least three months under compulsory supervision on release. In the case of juveniles who have served Section 53 sentences, the period of supervision may be longer, depending upon the stage in the sentence at which they were released. The supervising officer is either a probation officer, or a local authority social worker.

Secure training orders

Growing concern with a small number of juvenile offenders who allegedly commit a high number of offences led to provisions in the 1994 Criminal Justice and Public Order Act for sentencing 12–14-year-old persistent offenders to a secure training order. The new sentence will only apply to 12–14-year-old offenders who have been previously convicted of at least three imprisonable offences, of which at least one must have been committed whilst subject to the requirements of a supervision order. The court must also be satisfied that the offence is so serious as to warrant a custodial sentence or, in the case of a violent or sexual offence, that the public need to be protected from serious harm. Orders will be from six months to two years, with the first half being served in a secure training centre and the second half under compulsory supervision in the community. Breaches of supervision may result in the offender being readmitted to a secure training centre for up to a further three months. Currently, there are plans for five secure training centres across England, each offering about 40 places. The regimes will focus predominantly on providing education and training. The first secure training centres are scheduled to open in 1997.

Conclusions

Criminal justice in general, and juvenile or youth justice in particular, has undergone considerable change within the last four years. There have been three new pieces of legislation and a considerable number of related circulars, all of which have impacted on how young people are dealt with by the courts. The 1991 Act, close on the heels of the 1989 Children Act, concluded a move away from the simple welfare versus justice dichotomy and towards a system which is increasingly attempting to combine the benefits of both approaches into a consistent and more streamlined whole. This is perhaps illustrated in the most recent development within this field, namely the publication of a new consultation document on punishment in the community (Home Office 1995). This document, or green paper, is concerned with extending the court's discretion to determine the content of community sentences and combine their elements in a way which properly reflects both the seriousness of the offence and the suitability of the sentence for the individual offender.

The consultation document proposes the introduction of a single integrated community sentence to incorporate and replace all the current orders available in the adult court. It suggests that the courts should consider three main elements when passing community sentences – the restriction of liberty, reparation and the prevention of offending – and proposes a number of supplementary conditions, such as removing the current requirement that offenders consent to community orders. It remains to be seen what impact these proposals might have on the future of youth justice and the sentencing of young offenders.

References

Allen, R. (1991) Out of jail: the reduction in the use of penal custody for male juveniles 1981–88. *Howard Journal 30*, 1, 30–52.

Cavadino, P. and Gibson, B. (1993) *Bail: The Law, Best Practice and the Debate*. Winchester: Waterside Press.

Faulkner, D. (1995) Discretion in calling for pre-sentence reports. *The Magistrate 51*, 1, 12.

Gibson, B., Cavadino, P., Rutherford, A., Ashworth, A. and Harding, J. (1994) *The Youth Court: One Year Onwards*. Winchester: Waterside Press.

Home Affairs Select Committee (1993) *Report on Juvenile Offenders*. London: HMSO.

Home Office (1995) *Strengthening Punishment in the Community*. London: HMSO.

Royal Commission On Criminal Justice (1993) *Report of the Royal Commission on Criminal Justice*. London: HMSO.

Wilkinson, T. (1995) New rules for juvenile offenders. *Solicitors Journal* 10 February, 110–111.

Chapter 5

Children and Violence

Trauma in the American War Zone

James Garbarino and Kathleen Kostelny

Introduction: The American war zone

Violence is a fact of life for millions of American children. Homicide rates provide only an imprecise indicator of the overall problem of violence in the lives of American children and youth, for behind each murder stand many non-lethal assaults. The US Surgeon General's report in 1985 (Koop 1985) estimated 100 assaults for each murder. This ratio varies as a function of both medical trauma technology (which prevents assaults from becoming homicides) and weapons technology (which can increase or decrease the lethality of assaults). An example from Chicago illustrates this. The city's homicide rate in 1973 and 1993 was approximately the same, and yet the rate of serious assault increased approximately 400 per cent during that period. Thus, the ratio of assaults to homicides increased substantially.

Data from Chicago's Cook County Hospital provide another perspective on the changing nature of violence facing children in America. In 1982, the hospital responded to approximately 500 gunshot cases. In 1992 the number was approximately 1000. However, in 1982 almost all these cases involved single bullet injuries, while in 1992, 25 per cent involved multiple bullets. Rates of permanent disability have thus increased substantially, although the homicide rate has shown only a modest increase.

Class, race, and gender exert important influences on exposure to community violence. The odds of being a homicide victim range from 1:21 for Black males, to 1:369 for white females (with white males at 1:131, and Black females at 1:104) (Bell 1991). Being an American itself is a risk factor. The US far exceeds all other modern industrialised nations in its homicide rate (even for whites, where the rate of 11.2 per

100,000 is far more than the second place country, Scotland, with five per 100,000 (Richters and Martinez 1993).

Whatever the exact constellation of causes, children growing up in the United States have particularly high levels of exposure to violence. In three high risk neighbourhoods in Chicago, 17 per cent of the elementary school age children had witnessed domestic violence, 31 per cent had seen someone shot, and 84 per cent had seen someone 'beat up' (Bell 1991). Some 30 per cent of the kids living in high crime neighbourhoods of the cities like Chicago have witnessed a homicide by the time they are 15 years old, and more than 70 per cent have witnessed a serious assault. These figures are much more like the experience of kids in the war zones we have visited in other countries (Garbarino, Kostelny and Dubrow 1991) than they are of what we should expect for our own children, living in 'peace.' Richters and Martinez (1993) have amplified these results. In their study, 43 per cent of the fifth and sixth graders had witnessed a mugging in a 'moderately violent' neighbourhood in Washington, DC. Guns are one of the recurrent themes in the American war zone.

Listening to children: the gun culture

In our interviews with families living in public housing projects in Chicago we learned that virtually all the children had first-hand experiences with shooting by the time they were five years old (Dubrow and Garbarino 1989). Interviews with school-age children confirm that the 'gun culture' is a potent factor in the life of children in diverse settings in the United States (Garbarino 1995). The spread of the 'gun culture' into the lives of school children is associated with a clear and present danger to their mental health, social behaviour, and educational success. We base this conclusion upon an analysis of the role of trauma, threat, and violence on the development of children (Garbarino *et al.* 1992).

Perhaps a few examples will help illuminate the effects of this gun culture on the experience of childhood. In Detroit, a young boy whose idolised teenage brother was killed in a gang-related attack was asked, 'If you could have anything in the whole world, what would it be?' His answer: 'A gun so I could blow away the person that killed my brother' (Marin 1988). In California, when we asked a 9-year-old boy living in a neighbourhood characterised by declining security, 'What would it take to make you feel safer here?', he replied simply, 'If I had a gun of my own'. In a middle class suburb of Chicago, when we asked a classroom of 8-year-olds, 'If you needed a gun could you get one?', a third of the children were able to describe in detail how they would get one. In a prison in North Carolina, when we asked three incarcerated teenagers about why they had done the shooting that had landed them in prison, all three replied, 'What else was I supposed to do?'

We must understand the gun culture infusing the minds and hearts of American children and youth. Whether or not this cultural infusion results in actual shooting depends upon the particular circumstances of those children and youth, specifically, whether they experience an accumulation of social and psychological risk factors in the absence of compensatory opportunity factors.

The accumulation of risk

Risk accumulates. This is one of the conclusions we draw from our observations of children coping with chronic violence in today's America. Children are capable of coping with one or two major risk factors in their lives. But when risk accumulates – the addition of a third, fourth, and fifth risk factor – we see a precipitation of developmental damage (Sameroff *et. al.* 1987). This developmental model is particularly relevant to understanding the impact of chronic community violence on inner city children (Garbarino and Associates 1992).

The experience of community violence takes place within a larger context of risk for most children. They are often poor, live in father absent families, contend with parental incapacity due to depression or substance abuse, are raised by parents with little education or employment prospects, and are exposed to domestic violence (Kotlowitz 1991).

This constellation of risk by itself creates enormous challenges for young children. For them, the trauma of community violence is often literally 'the straw that breaks the camel's back'. Bearing in mind that approximately 20 per cent of American children live with this sort of accumulation of risk, the problem of violence is clearly a national problem with far reaching implications for child development.

The task of dealing with the effects of this environmental conspiracy falls to the people who care for these children – their parents and other relatives, teachers, and counsellors. But these adults take on this task facing enormous challenges of their own. We have found that human service professionals and educators working in the high violence areas of our communities are themselves traumatised by their exposure to violence.

In one study we found that 60 per cent of the Head Start staff members surveyed in Chicago had experienced traumatic events connected with violence (Garbarino *et al.* 1992). For these individuals efforts to create a 'safe zone' in the school are crucial to their ability to perform their important functions in the lives of high risk children. For this safe zone to help children focus on their school work it must exist as part of their 'social maps'.

The social maps of children in danger

Certainly one of the most important features of child development is the child's emerging capacity to form and maintain 'social maps' (Garbarino and Associates 1992). These representations of the world reflect the simple cognitive competence of the child (knowing the world in the scientific sense of objective, empirical fact), to be sure. But they also indicate the child's moral and affective inclination.

We are concerned with the conclusions about the world contained in the child's social maps: 'adults are to be trusted because they know what they are doing', 'people will generally treat you well and meet your needs', 'strangers are dangerous', 'school is a safe place'. The forces shaping these maps include the child's experiences in counterpoint with the child's inner life – both the cognitive competence and the working of unconscious forces.

Young children must contend with dangers that derive from two sources not nearly so relevant to adults. First, their physical immaturity places them at risk for injury from trauma that would not hurt adults because they are larger and more powerful. Second, young children tend to believe in the reality of threats from what most adults would define as 'the fantasy' world. This increases their vulnerability to perceiving themselves as being 'in danger'. These dangers include monsters under the bed, wolves in the basement, and invisible creatures that lurk in the dark corners of bedrooms.

Trauma arises when the child cannot give meaning to dangerous experiences. This orientation is contained in the American Psychiatric Association's definition of Post-Traumatic Stress Disorder, which refers to threatening experiences outside the realm of normal experience.

Herman defined trauma thus: to come face to face with both human vulnerability in the natural world and with the capacity for evil in human nature (Herman 1992).

This suggests experiences which are cognitively overwhelming in which the process required to 'understand' these experiences has pathogenic side effects. That is, in coping with traumatic events, the child is forced into patterns of behaviour, thought, and feelings that are themselves 'abnormal' when contrasted with that of the untraumatised healthy child. Children are particularly vulnerable to the trauma caused by threat and fear – those exposed to trauma before age 10 were three times for likely to exhibit PTSD than those exposed after age 12 in one study (Davidson and Smith 1990).

Children and youth exposed to acute danger may require processing over a period of months (Pynoos and Nadar 1988). And, if the traumatic stress is intense enough, it may leave permanent 'psychic scars' (Terr 1990). This is particularly the case for children made vulnerable because of disruptions in their primary relationships (most notably with parents). These effects include excessive sensitivity to stimuli associated with the trauma and diminished expectations for the future (Terr 1990).

But chronic danger imposes a requirement for *developmental* adjustment – *accommodations*. These are likely to include persistent Post-Traumatic Stress Syndrome, alterations of personality, and major changes in patterns of behaviour or articulation of ideological interpretations of the world that provide a framework for making sense of on going danger (Garbarino *et al.* 1992). This is particularly true when that danger comes from violent overthrow of day-to-day social reality, as is the case in war, communal violence, or chronic violent crime.

Beyond any individual strengths that come to a child with temperament and intellectual capacity at birth, the key lies in the balance of social supports from and for parents. It lies in parental capacity to buffer social stress in the lives of children and offering them a positive path to follow in dealing with that stress. The quality of life for young children – and their reservoirs of resilience – thus becomes a social indicator as well as a measure of personal worth. This hypothesis emerges from a wide range of research and clinical observation.

Adults as teachers

Adults are crucial resources for children attempting to cope with chronic danger and stress. Generations of studies focusing on the experience of children living in war zones testify to the importance of adult responses to danger as mediating factors in child response (Garbarino *et al.* 1991). So long as adults take charge of themselves and present children with a role model of calm, positive determination, most children can cope with a great deal of chronic stress associated with community violence. They may indeed be traumatised by their experiences, but the adults around them will be able to serve as a resource and support the child in rehabilitative efforts.

However, once adults begin to deteriorate, to decompensate, to panic, children suffer. This is not surprising, given the importance of the images of adults contained in the child's social maps. Traumatised children need help to recover from their experiences (Terr 1990). Emotionally disabled or immobilised adults are unlikely to offer the children what they need. Such adults are inclined to engage in denial, to be emotionally inaccessible, and are prone to misinterpret the child's signals. Messages of safety are particularly important in establishing adults as sources of protection and authority for children living in conditions of threat and violence.

In Vygotsky's approach (1986), child development is fundamentally *social*: cognitive development proceeds at its best through the process of interactive teaching. He focuses on the Zone of Proximal Development: the difference between what the child can accomplish alone versus what the child can accomplish with the guidance of the teacher. How is this relevant to the child's ability to cope with trauma?

In the case of acute trauma (a single horrible incident that violates the normal reality of the child's world) the child needs help believing that 'things are back to normal'. This is a relatively easy teaching task, this therapy of reassurance. But the child who lives with chronic trauma (for example, the problem of community violence) needs something more. This child needs to be taught how to redefine the world in moral and structural terms.

The child needs assistance in 'processing' the existing world if that child is to avoid drawing social and/or psychologically pathogenic conclusions: 'the world is a hostile and dangerous place', 'adults have lost control of the world', 'kill or be killed', 'don't trust anyone', 'my enemies are less than human'. Here the role of the adult as teacher is crucial for the well-being of the child and for well being of the community in which that child is to be a citizen.

Consequences of growing up in a war zone

Many inner city children are experiencing the symptoms of Post-Traumatic Stress Disorder, symptoms which include sleep disturbances, day dreaming, recreating trauma in play, extreme startle responses, emotional numbing, diminished expectations for the future, and even biochemical changes in their brains that impair social and academic behaviour. This trauma can produce significant psychological problems that interfere with learning and appropriate social behaviour in school and that interfere with normal parent–child relationships.

Trauma and its consequences can also make them prime candidates for involvement in gangs. The violent economy of the illicit drug trade offers a sense of belonging and solidarity as well as cash income for kids who have few pro-social alternatives for either. The peer alliances offer some sense of security in a hostile world. If these children do not develop a sense of confidence that adults are committed to providing a safe zone, their willingness and ability to take advantage of developmental opportunities will decrease and this will adversely affect their future.

Based upon our work in the field and our understanding of the research and clinical experience of our colleagues, we have reached the conclusion that there are many similarities between the experiences of children growing up in war zones around the world and American children growing up amidst chronic community violence. These similarities hit home for us particularly in comparing the situation of children in refugee camps we have visited in Thailand, Hong Kong, and the Middle East, and public housing projects in Chicago and other cities.

In both the camps and the projects, there is a proliferation of weapons – a kind of 'arms race' – which exacerbates the effects of conflict and violence. It is common for young people – particularly males – to be heavily armed and to be engaged in armed attacks and reprisals. Substantial numbers of 'bystander' injuries are observed.

In both the camps and the projects, representatives of 'mainstream' society have only partial control over what happens. The international relief workers leave the camps at the end of the working day, and so do the social workers and educators in the public housing projects. Both the camps and the projects are under the control of the local gangs at night. Therefore, no action during the day can succeed unless it is acceptable to the gangs that rule the community at night. For example, there have been cases in public housing projects in Chicago in which local gangs have established curfews on their own initiative and in which gangs make the decision about whether or not someone who commits a crime against residents will be identified and punished.

In both the camps and the projects, women – particularly mothers – are in a desperate situation. They are under enormous stress, often are the target of domestic violence, and have few economic or educational resources and prospects. Men play a marginal role in the enduring life of families – being absent for reasons that include participating in the fighting, fleeing to escape enemies, being injured or killed, and (particularly in the case of the American public housing project), being imprisoned. Largely as a result, there is a major problem of maternal depression. Studies in both settings have reported 50 per cent of the women being seriously depressed.

In both the camps and the projects, one consequence of maternal depression is neglect of children. This connection is well established in research. This neglect leads to elevated levels of 'accidental injuries' to children as well as a more generalised lack of psychological availability.

In both the camps and the projects, children and youth have diminished prospects for the future. This lack of a positive future orientation produces depression, rage, and disregard for human life – their own and others.

One focus of international initiatives (such as the UN Convention on the Rights of the Child) is to create 'zones of peace' for children, and generally to encourage combatants to institute and respect protected areas for children. Violence free zones in and around schools are a logical parallel relevant to the United States. Underlying all such efforts is an attempt to communicate a message of safety to children, to stimulate a redrawing of their social maps.

International action does bring change for families living in refugee camps, however. For example, the signing of a peace accord has meant that repatriation has come to the Khmer, and they are returning to Cambodia to take up a more genuine community life. However, without some comparable national effort to achieve reconciliation, social justice, and a major peacekeeping force in our cities, most of the families in America's urban war zones will remain there, and another generation of children will experience the trauma of chronic community violence. Therein lies one major difference for children living in the world's refugee camps and children living in many of America's public housing projects. In war zones, there is hope of peace, repatriation, and the renewal of community life. In the case of community violence in America, the war never ends, peace never comes.

Our efforts to understand the impact of chronic community violence on children and youth around the world and in our own cities highlights several concerns – unmet medical needs, the corrosive effects of the co-experiencing of poverty and violence on personality and on academic achievement, etc. But from our perspective, *the most important of these is that the experience of trauma distorts the values of kids*. Unless we reach them with healing experiences and offer them a moral and political framework within which to process their experiences, *traumatised kids are likely to be drawn to groups and ideologies that legitimise and reward their rage, their fear, and their hateful cynicism*. This is an environment in which gangs flourish and community institutions deteriorate.

At the heart of this downward spiral is declining trust in adults on the part of children and youth in high-violence communities. As one youth living in a small city experiencing a proliferation of gangs put it to us recently: 'If I join a gang I will be 50 per cent safe, but if I don't I will be 0 per cent safe.' He does not put his trust and faith in adults. That is what he is telling us if we are prepared to listen. There are self-serving, anti-social individuals and groups in our society prepared to mobilise and exploit the anger, fear, alienation, and hostility that many kids feel. *They* are listening. Are *we*?

References

Bell, C. (1991) Traumatic stress and children in danger. *Journal of Health Care for the Poor and Underserved* 2, 1, 175–88.

Davidson, J. and Smith, R. (1990) Traumatic experiences in psychiatric outpatients. *Journal of Traumatic Stress* 3, 3, 459–475.

Dubrow, N.F. and Garbarino, J. (1989) Living in a war zone: mothers and young children in a public housing development. *Child Welfare* 68, 1, 3–20.

Garbarino, J. (1990) Youth in dangerous environments: coping with the consequences. In K. Hurrelmann and F. Losel (eds) *Health Hazards in Adolescence*. New York: Walter de Gruyter.

Garbarino, J. and Associated (1992) *Children and Families in the Social Environment.* New York: Aldine DeGruyter.

Garbarino, J. (1995) *Raising Children in a Socially Toxic Environment.* San Francisco, CA: Jossey-Bass.

Garbarino, J., Guttmann, E. and Seeley, J. (1986) *The Psychologically Battered Child.* San Francisco: Jossey-Bass.

Garbarino, J., Kostelny, K. and Dubrow, N. (1991) *No Place to Be a Child: Growing Up in a War Zone.* Lexington, Massachusetts: Lexington Books.

Garbarino, J., Dubrow, N., Kostelny, K. and Pardo, C. (1992) *Children in Danger: Coping with the Consequences.* San Francisco: Jossey-Bass.

Herman, R. (1992) *Trauma and Recovery.* New York: Basic Books.

Koop, E. (1985) *Report of the Surgeon General.* Washington, DC: US Public Health Service.

Kotlowitz, A. (1991) *There are no Children Here. The Story of Two Boys Growing Up in the Other America.* New York: Doubleday.

Losel, F. and Bliesener, T. (1990) Resilience in adolescence: a study on the generalizability of protective factors. In K. Hurrelmann and F. Losel (eds) *Health Hazards in Adolescence.* New York: Walter de Gruyter.

Marin, (1988) 'Grief's Children.' Documentary, WMAQ News, Chicago, June 21, 1988.

Pynoos, R. and Nader, K. (1988) Psychological first aid and treatment approach to children exposed to community violence: research implications. *Journal of Traumatic Stress 1,* 445–473.

Richters, J.E. and Martinez, P. (1993) The NIMH community violence project: I. children as victims of and witnesses to violence. *Psychiatry Interpersonal and Biological Processes 56,* 1, 7–21.

Sameroff, A., Seifer, R., Barocas, R., Zax, M. and Greenspan, S. (1987) Intelligent quotient scores of 4-year-old children: social environment risk factors. *Pediatrics 79, 3,* 343–350.

Terr, L. (1990) *Too Scared to Cry.* New York: Harper and Row.

Vygotsky, L. (1986) *Thought and Language.* Cambridge, MA: MIT Press.

Chapter 6

Female Offenders in Scotland

Implications for Theory[1 2]

Elaine Samuel and Kay Tisdall

Introduction

In the past 15 years, a wealth of feminist-inspired literature has emerged on women in the criminal justice system. Throughout this literature is a constant refrain – girls and women who offend have all but been ignored in the criminological literature (Campbell 1991; Eaton 1987; Edwards 1989; Genders and Player 1986; Heidensohn 1987; Petrie 1986; Shelden and Chesney-Lind 1993). Certainly, more men are involved in the criminal justice system than women. But this only makes the gender issue more pertinent. First, the gender differential in offending may help us understand why some people rather than others become involved in criminal activities. Second, the difference may point to ways of dealing with criminality. As Heidensohn has herself suggested:

> ...far more women than men are successfully held back by social controls and fears of social reaction...The answer to football hooligans might not then be identity cards, barbed wire enclosures or life sentences but rather the feminisation of socialisation. (1987, pp. 25–26)

The message of feminist criminology to criminologists, then, is: ignore gender issues at your peril.

This does not mean to say that women are not mentioned in the past 100 years of criminological literature. Indeed, landmark texts in the

---

1 This chapter is an updated extract from Samuel 1994.

2 The authors appreciate the provision of statistical data by the Scottish Office Home and Health Department.

literature, such as it is, have been very influential. Lombroso and Ferrero (1895) understood criminality in evolutionary terms. Female criminals were 'pseudo-males,' genetic throw-backs to the time when women were not fully differentiated from men. Women generally did not commit crime, according to these writers, because they were less intelligent, had less abstract reasoning capacity and were passive by nature. Psychosocial arguments emerged in the early 20th century, with female offenders being labelled as maladjusted: that is, using their sexuality in socially unacceptable ways such as law-breaking in order to gain the social approval and affection which all girls and women craved (see Thomas 1923). Pollak's work in the 1950s combined biological and cultural influences to assert that women were equally as criminal as men, but women committed their crimes in different ways, were essentially deceitful, and thus escaped detection. Further, if women offenders were detected, they were treated more leniently by law enforcement due to the 'chivalry factor':

> This attitude exists on the part of the male victim of crime as well as on the part of the officers of the law, who are still largely male in our society. Men hate to accuse women and thus indirectly to send them to their punishment, police officers dislike to arrest them, district attorneys to prosecute them, judges and juries to find them guilty, and so on. (Pollak 1950, p.151)

Thus, three critical and influential ideas have permeated the discourse on female offending: that female offenders are innately irrational and immoral (whether through weakness or as 'evil' women), they are in special need of protection, particularly from their own sexuality, and they meet with greater leniency and protectionism from the criminal justice system (the 'chivalry factor'). This may be contrasted to male offenders, and particularly young men, for whom criminality is often perceived to be common, normal and natural – a stage of life which they will generally outgrow.

Second-wave feminists in the 1970s investigated the purported greater leniency towards female offenders in the criminal justice system. While more lenient sentencing for female offenders was initially found (for example, see Nagel and Weitzman 1971), doubts were later cast on empirical research that did not consider key legal variables, such as previous record and seriousness of offence. When these variables were considered, differences between male and female offenders largely disappeared in sentencing for the same offences (Eaton 1986, p.12, 1987, pp.95 and 98; Edwards 1989, p.169; Farrington and Morris 1983; Steffensmeier, Kramer and Streifel 1993, p.412). Certain criminologists (see Adler 1975) thought that women's crime would gradually converge with men's crime – both in numbers and types of offending – due to the women's movement and greater equality.

Mirroring the growing sophistication of feminist theory, in the 1980s the response of the criminal justice system to female offending was examined with greater sensitivity to its complexities. Other gender-related variables, such as the influence of domestic status, were considered. Edwards (1989) found, for example, that 'where judicial personnel could see women were already under the constraints imposed by economic dependency, marriage and family responsibilities...they were likely to be treated more leniently than were men and women of a less conventional kind' (pp. 176–177). Gender was seen to interact with other factors such as race and class so that 'the majority of criminalised and imprisoned females are victims of typifications that discriminate primarily against working-class and black women' (Carlen and Worrall 1987, p.8). Recent literature on female offending suggests that women who offend can be seen as doubly deviant:

> ...as rare, abnormal female offenders for breaking social rules and as 'unfeminine and unnatural' women who have broken out of their conventional roles. (Heidensohn 1987, p.20)

Moreover, when women committed stereotypically 'masculine' crimes such as assaults, robbery and other violent acts, they were even more likely to be perceived as 'unfeminine and unnatural'. They became triply deviant: they had broken laws, broken away from the 'feminine' role by offending and, in these cases, by their type of offending. These women might therefore be treated more harshly than women who committed stereotypically 'feminine' crimes such as shoplifting and more harshly than men who committed the same crimes (Willemsen and van Schie 1989). In sum, while chivalry may be extended to some female offenders by the criminal justice system, research suggests it only extends so far as their class, race, domestic situation and offence are 'chivalry-appropriate' (Samuel 1994).

Though more careful analysis appears to have erased statistical support for the 'chivalry factor' affecting adult women as a group, research does suggest that the 'chivalry factor' does affect young women. Rather than leniency, however, the protectionism inherent to the 'chivalry factor' leads to greater social control. Chesney-Lind, for example, has written copiously on the harsher treatment of girls for 'status' offences – activities which would not be considered criminal for adults, such as running away – compared to boys, in the United States (see 1988 and 1993). In their reviews of the literature, both Campbell (1981) and Heidensohn (1987) note evidence to suggest greater interference by the criminal justice system in the lives of girls than boys, particularly for trivial offences.

In this chapter, the applicability of these themes will be assessed for girls and young women in Scotland, through an examination of official statistics. At present, no major study exists as to the involvement of female offenders in the Scottish criminal justice system. What does exist is official statistics collected for other purposes. Since the statistics were not gathered specifically to answer the questions posed here, they provide the usual mix of illumination and frustration. Comparisons are not consistently made across statistics by gender; key legal criteria, such as criminal record and severity of offence, are not always available. Further, the usual qualifications in regards to official criminal statistics apply. For example, official statistics do not come near to replicating the actual number of offences nor the full extent of action taken by the criminal justice system. Despite these gaps, the Scottish criminological literature has so rarely addressed the question of female offenders within the Scottish criminal justice system (for discussion, see Asquith *et al.* 1995; Samuel 1994) that a basic analysis is useful, if only to raise more questions as to the response of the criminal justice system to female offending than can presently be answered.

Gender and crime

As the literature would suggest, considerably more men than women are found guilty of crimes and offences in Scotland. In 1993, 160,324 people in Scotland had a charge proved against them for crimes or offences.[3 4] Only 16 per cent of these people were female. Women have gradually increased their proportion of people with charges proved in the past five years and, more inconsistently, increased in the number of people with charges proved. These patterns run contrary to charges proved against men, and charges proved against both sexes: the number of charges proved against men has decreased in the past five years by 8.3 per cent and the overall number of charges proved has dropped by 6.3 per cent (see Table 6.1).

Table 6.1 People[1] with charges proved (Scotland 1989–1993[2])

All crimes and offences, by main charge proved	*Number*			*Per cent (%)*	
	Males	*Females*	*All[1]*	*Male*	*Female*
1989	147,660	23,006	171,163	86	13
1990	149,545	24,194	173,924	86	14
1991	142,788	25,484	168,382	85	15
1992	146,554	27,783	174,353	84	16
1993	135,156	25,113	160,324	84	16

Notes:
1 Includes those people whose sex is not known and excludes companies.
2 Note that 1988–1990 statistics were revised in Scottish Office 1992, following the discovery of programming errors.
Source: Scottish Office 1992, 1993 and 1994b, Tables 8.

These general trends are repeated when charges proved are examined by crimes and offences. However, the trends are more pronounced in regards to offences, rather than crimes (see Tables 6.2 and 6.3).

3 Note that official Scottish statistics are for 'main charge proved'. Where a person is proceeding against for more than one crime or offence, only the main charge is counted. For further information, see statistical note 2 in Scottish Office 1994b.
4 The Scottish Office divides contraventions of the law into crimes and offences, crimes generally being the more serious. For further information, see statistical note 19 in Scottish Office 1994b.

Table 6.2 People[1] with charges proved for crimes (Scotland 1989–1993[2])

All crimes and offences, by main charge proved	*Number*			*Per cent (%)*	
	Males	*Females*	*All[1]*	*Male*	*Female*
1989	45,928	7211	53,320	86	14
1990	45,638	7686	53,399	85	14
1991	42,364	7149	49,564	85	14
1992	46,378	7000	54,315	85	15
1993	44,376	7891	52,293	85	15

Notes:
1 Includes those people whose sex is not known and excludes companies.
2 Note that 1988–1990 statistics were revised in Scottish Office 1992, following the discovery of programming errors.
Source: Scottish Office 1992, 1993 and 1994b, Tables 8.

Table 6.3 People[1] with charges proved for offences (Scotland 1989–1993[2])

All crimes and offences, by main charge proved	*Number*			*Per cent (%)*	
	Males	*Females*	*All[1]*	*Male*	*Female*
1989	101,732	15,795	117,843	86	13
1990	103,907	16,508	120,525	86	13
1991	100,424	18,335	118,818	85	15
1992	100,176	19,900	120,140	83	17
1993	90,780	17,222	108,031	84	16

Notes:
1 Includes those people whose sex is not known and excludes companies.
2 Note that 1988–1990 statistics were revised in Scottish Office 1992, following the discovery of programming errors.
Source: Scottish Office 1992, 1993 and 1994b, Tables 8.

Women are thus increasing their proportion and number of charges proved in the less serious law-breaking offences.

What type of offences and crimes are women committing? Has this changed in the past five years? The eight most common charges proved against women in 1993 are compared in Table 6.4 with the numbers in 1989.

Table 6.4 Number of women with charges proved, by eight most common charges proved against women, in 1989 and 1993 (Scotland 1989[1] and 1993)

	Number		*Per cent of main charges proved against women (%)*	
Main charge proved	*1989*	*1993*	*1989*	*1993*
1 'Other' miscellaneous offences (including TV licence)	7005	7908	30	31
2 Shoplifting	1948	2400	8	10
3 Unlawful use of vehicle	1482	2020	6	8
4 Breach of the peace	1807	1616	8	6
5 Speeding	1053	1467	5	6
6 Simple assault	1289	1291	6	5
7 'Other' theft (includes forgery, embezzlement, and reset)	1738	1214	8	5
8 'Other' motor vehicle offences (including parking, neglect of traffic directions)	1088	1127	5	5

Note:
1 Note that 1989 statistics were revised in Scottish Office 1992, following the discovery of programming errors.
Source: Scottish Office 1992 and 1994b, Tables 8.

Female offenders are most involved in minor charges as their main charges, with only 'other' theft and shoplifting as crimes rather than offences – as would be anticipated from Table 6.4. The same top eight offences for women are repeated from 1989 to 1993, with some slight changes in rank orders. The more physical offences (breach of the peace and simple assault) decreased slightly, while shoplifting had a slight rise. Men similarly are most often charged with offences, with 'other' theft and crimes against public justice as their only crimes in their top eight number of main charges proved. From most common to least, men's eight most numerous main charges in 1993 were: unlawful use of vehicle (14%); breach of the peace (12%); speeding (10%); simple assault (8%); 'other' miscellaneous offences (6%); 'other' motor vehicle offences (6%); drunk driving (5%); 'other' theft (4%); and crimes against public justice (4%). While 'other' miscellaneous offences was nearly one-third of all female offences, men's most common charge proved (unlawful use of vehicle) was only 14% of men's total charges proved.

Whether these statistics confirm that female emancipation is leading to convergence between women's and men's criminality is debatable. Charges are more often being proved against women than in the past, while charges proved for the population as a whole are decreasing. Yet the increase has primarily been for more minor offences, rather than crimes. Rather than convergence due to women becoming 'more like men', women may have both more opportunity and more need to offend (for example, see Carlen and Worrall 1987; Steffensmeier, Allan and Streifel 1989): statements well-represented by the increased part-time employment by women, increasing number of single-parent families and increasing poverty in Scotland (Tisdall with Donaghie 1995).

Age, gender and crime

Commonly held assumptions about female delinquency lack the age perspective of male delinquency. Young men are believed to offend because of their youth and it is expected that their offending behaviour will decrease with age. Female offenders, on the other hand, are seen as in some way pathological, and offending rates would be expected to be independent of age. However, Scottish statistics (Table 6.5) do not support this description of female offending.

Measured by charges proved for crimes, breach of the peace and petty assault, both women's and men's offending have peak ages: offending increases when people are young and then decreases substantially (a finding similar to that found by Eisenman and Kritsonis (1993) in the United States). Both men and women as a group now peak at the same age, 18 years. The rate of conviction for Scottish women shows a substantial decline between the ages of 20 and 45, but not as dramatic a decline as for men. The data does demonstrate that, for both women and men, crime is very much a youth related phenomenon in Scotland.

Table 6.5 Individuals with at least one charge proved for crimes, petty assault and breach of the peace (Scotland 1993)

	Rate per 10,000 population	
Age	*Males*	*Females*
15	17	2
16	324	52
17	764	122
18	960	130
19	957	109
20	844	111
25	517	83
30	326	63
35	216	47
40	157	34
45	103	20

Source: Scottish Office 1995.

Leniency and control

The literature reported in the introduction suggests that, on aggregate, official criminal justice statistics appear to show greater leniency in sentencing towards women. The more recent literature, however, finds that legal criteria – such as type of offence, seriousness of offence and criminal record – erase the purported leniency caused by the 'chivalry factor'. As we have noted, researchers such as Chesney-Lind in the United States assert that girls and young women are not treated more leniently. Rather, the criminal justice system seeks to exert greater social control in order to 'protect' them.

The Scottish criminal justice system, however, has a clear alternative route from the court system for most offences for children who offend – the Children's Hearing System. Many of the 'status offences' identified by Chesney-Lind (such as running away) are dealt with through the Children's Hearings System rather than the courts. The children's hearings are based on the welfare principle, and leave decisions of guilt to the courts. Thus, a greater use of the children's hearings for young females who offend could demonstrate greater protectionism (for discussion of 'net-widening', see Samuel 1994).

What evidence can be found in Scottish official statistics of greater leniency or control towards young girls and women? Can this be explained away by legal criteria? The following section will seek to answer these questions by looking at criminal statistics for children from the age of 8 to 16 (the age of criminal responsibility in Scotland is 8), and young people from the ages of 16 to 20. While some data can be found on type of offence and criminal record, no data are readily available on the seriousness of offence within an offence type. Data for children (on initial police actions on initial reports) are only available up to 1989 in Scotland, as collection of the statistics was then discontinued.

Children

Official police actions on initial reports[5] provide some evidence of greater leniency for girls. In Scotland, police can take at least three official actions against children: they can officially warn the children; they can refer the matter to the Reporter, who is part of the Scottish Children's Hearings System; or they can refer the matter to the Procurator Fiscal, who can then decide to refer to the Reporter or (rarely) to prosecute. Informal warnings by the police are not included in official statistics. Of all children against whom some official police action was taken, the following percentages of girls and boys (Table 6.6) were warned or referred:

Table 6.6 Initial police reports for children[1] (Scotland 1989)

All actions	*Warning*	*Referral to Reporter*	*Referral to Procurator Fiscal*
Boys (100%) (N= 23,400)	10%	77%	13%
Girls (100%) (N= 2936)	19%	69%	12%

Note:
1 Children are defined as: people aged 8 to 16 and those aged under 18 who are under a supervision requirement from a children's hearing.
Source: Scottish Office 1991b, Table 5.

5 Note that one report can cover more than one offence, and the police judge the most serious offence for the official statistics.

Thus, girls were almost twice as likely to receive an official warning than boys. A greater proportion of boys, than girls, are referred to the welfare-based children's hearings system; almost equal proportions of boys and girls are referred to the justice-based court system through the Procurator Fiscal.[6] Judging by this division, the statistics do not demonstrate that welfare concerns will predominate for female offenders and justice concerns for male offenders.

Campbell (1981) and Carlen (1987) suggest that girls' offending is 'sexualised' after they reach puberty, and that the criminal justice system is more paternal – and thus more protectionist and interventionist – for girls than boys. When children are 15, however, the patterns appear only more pronounced, showing greater leniency to girls rather than greater protectionism at this stage of police action (Table 6.7).

Table 6.7 Initial police reports for children aged 15 (Scotland 1989)

All actions	*Warning*	*Referral to Reporter*	*Referral to Procurator Fiscal*
Boys (100%)[1] (N= 8854)	5%	73%	21%
Girls (100%) (N= 1087)	14%	67%	18%

Note:

1 Note that due to rounding on percentages, total for this row does not equal 100.

Source: Scottish Office 1991a, Table 5.

At age 15, both boys and girls are less likely to receive an official warning than children of all ages. Fifteen year old girls, however, are almost three times as likely to receive a warning than boys. They are only slightly less likely than boys to be referred to the Procurator Fiscal. Some evidence for leniency on aggregate exists, once an initial police report is made, but only at the lower end of the tariff for girls.

TYPE OF OFFENDING

Can such aggregate leniency be accounted for by legal criteria, such as type of offending behaviour, the seriousness of the offence or previous criminal record, rather than 'chivalry' on the part of the police? Con-

6 Note that offences at a certain level of seriousness must be reported to the Procurator Fiscal.

clusive data are not available, although data provide some suggestions as to the effects of main offence type.

Initial police reports can be compared by type of offence and sex, keeping the age of the offender constant. For example, comparisons can be made for young people at the age of 15 years. Of the 1087 15-year-old girls on whom police filed reports in Scotland in 1989, 71 per cent of all offences were for shoplifting, petty assault, breach of the peace and other theft. Comparing formal police response to boys' and girls' offending behaviour, girls were almost twice as likely to receive a warning than boys on each of these offences. At the same time, they were almost as likely as boys to be referred to the Procurator Fiscal or the Reporter on each of these offences (Table 6.8).

Table 6.8 Initial police reports, by four offences most commonly brought against girls age 15 (Scotland 1989)

	Per cent (%)		
All actions	*Warning*	*Referral to Reporter*	*Referral to Procurator Fiscal*
Shoplifting			
Boys (100%) (N=651)	12	71	17
Girls (100%) (N=249)	20	64	16
Petty Assault			
Boys (100%) (N=866)	6	77	17
Girls (100%) (N=237)	11	75	14
Breach of the Peace			
Boys (100%) (N=1580)	6	77	17
Girls (100%) (N=189)	12	72	16
Other Theft			
Boys (100%) (N=986)	5	78	17
Girls (100%) (N=93)	10	74	16

Source: Scottish Office 1995.

Thus, the overall tendency for girls to be treated more leniently at the lower end of the tariff cannot be substantially explained by type of offence alone, though there may be differences between boys and girls in the gravity of their behaviour within an offence type as well as previous offending behaviour.

Young adults

The sentencing structure of young adults may be subjected to a similar analysis. Generally, probation is considered a 'welfare' option, combining both care and control (Webb 1984), whereas Community Service Orders are 'no easy option' and are considered a 'justice' alternative to custody (Table 6.9).

Table 6.9 Young adults (16–20 years old) with charges proved by main penalty (Scotland 1993)

Main penalty	*Per cent (%)*					
	Other[1]	*Admonishment/ caution*	*Fine*	*Probation*	*Community Service Order (CSO)*	*Custody*
Males (100%) (N=32,268)	3	13	58	7	6	13
Females (100%) (N=3541)	3	26	58	7	2	4

Note:

1 'Other' includes 2% compensation orders and 1% absolute discharge for both sexes.

Source: Scottish Office 1994b, Table 13.

At the extreme ends of the sentencing tariff, young women were clearly treated more leniently on aggregate. Young men in Scotland in 1993 were more than three times as likely as women to be sentenced to custody, and half as likely to be admonished or cautioned. Young men were three times as likely as young women to be referred for a Community Service Order. In the middle of the sentencing tariff, young women now equally receive fines and probation when charges are proven. In a significant shift, young women now are as likely to receive the 'welfare' option of probation as young men, whereas in 1990 young women were twice as likely to receive probation (Scottish Office 1992).

TYPE OF OFFENDING

The picture does not change significantly when the nature of female offending behaviour is taken into consideration and sentencing controlled for type of offence. In 1993, 59 per cent of all charges against young adult women were accounted for by shoplifting, 'other' miscellaneous offences, simple assault, breach of the peace, and 'other' theft (Table 6.10) (Scottish Office 1995).

Table 6.10 Young adults (16–20 years old) with charges proved on the five most common main charges proved for young women, by penalties (Scotland 1993)

Main penalty	*Per cent (%)*					
	Other[1]	*Admonishment/ caution*	*Fine*	*Probation*	*Community Service Order (CSO)*	*Custody*
Shoplifting						
Males (100%) (N=1173)	1	18	53	9	3	16
Females (100%) (N=583)	1	33	47	9	3	6
'Other' miscellaneous offences						
Males (100%) (N=1602)	1	11	35	14	8	30
Females (100%) (N=458)	1	17	74	3	1	3
Simple assault						
Males (100%) (N=2594)	4	13	59	6	7	11
Females (100%) (N=427)	6	37	42	7	4	4
Breach of the peace						
Males (100%) (N=4081)	1	21	71	2	1	3
Females (100%) (N=334)	2	44	46	4	1	3
'Other' theft						
Males (100%) (N=2067)	5	18	48	10	7	12
Females (100%) (N=290)	4	27	51	9	2	7

Note:

1 'Other' includes compensation orders and absolute discharge for both sexes. All rows do not add to 100% due to rounding of percentages.

Source: Scottish Office 1995.

The differential sentencing rates appear largely to repeat themselves. Some differences are noted, however. For example, rather than equally receiving fines for shoplifting or breach of the peace, young women are as likely as young men to receive the harsher disposal of a Community Service Order and, for breach of the peace, custody. For 'other' miscellaneous offences, rather than equally receiving probation, young women are nearly twice as likely to receive fines than young men and dramatically less likely to receive custody. The category of 'other' miscellaneous offences, however, covers a wide variety of offences and thus differences within this offence type may explain the differences in penalties. Overall, when young women are penalised for crimes or offences that are most likely to be committed by their female peers, they are typically not treated the same as young men committing the same crimes or offences. This is true particularly at the lower end of the sentencing tariff. On first appearance, therefore, type of offending does not account for, nor explain away, gender differentials found in the aggregate sentencing data.

CRIMINAL RECORD

Data are available on the number of convictions any individual receives in a single year, although not on individuals' full criminal records. If we examine penalties imposed on 16–20-year-olds in Scotland, who were only convicted once in 1993 of crimes, breach of the peace and simple assault, a similar – and perhaps even exaggerated – pattern is evident. Young women are nearly twice as likely as young men to

Table 6.11 Young adults (16–20 years old) with a single conviction during the year for crimes, breach of the peace and simple assault (Scotland 1993)

	Per cent (%)					
Main penalty	*Other*[1]	*Admonishment/ caution*	*Fine*	*Probation*	*Community Service Order (CSO)*	*Custody*
Males (100%) (N=8580)	5	18	63	4	6	5
Females (100%) (N=1314)	6	36	50	4	2	1

Note:

1 'Other' includes compensation orders and absolute discharge. All rows do not add to 100% due to rounding of percentages.

Source: Scottish Office 1995.

receive an admonishment or caution and less like to receive a fine. At the same time, young men are three times more likely to receive a Community Service Order and five times more likely to be given a custodial sentence (Table 6.11).

Is the greater leniency displayed towards young women explained when types of offences they have committed are taken into account? While statistics are not available on the severity of the crime/offence within the type of crime/offence, the types of crimes/offences do not support such an explanation (Table 6.12).

Table 6.12 Young adults (16–20 years old) with charges proved on the four most common main charges proved for young women with a single conviction in the past year, for a crime, breach of the peace or simple assault, by penalties (Scotland 1993)

	Per cent (%)					
Main penalty	*Other*[1]	*Admonish-ment/ caution*	*Fine*	*Probation*	*Community Service Order (CSO)*	*Custody*
Simple Assault						
Males (100%) (N=1185)	4	17	66	3	6	3
Females (100%) (N=277)	8	44	12	4	2	–
Shoplifting						
Males (100%) (N=246)	1	27	64	2	2	4
Females (100%) (N=245)	3	40	53	2	1	<0
Breach of the peace						
Males (100%) (N=1782)	2	26	70	1	1	<0
Females (100%) (N=188)	3	51	45	1	–	–
'Other' theft						
Males (100%) (N=755)	6	24	59	5	5	2
Females (100%) (N= 160)	7	28	58	6	1	–

Note:

1 'Other' includes compensation orders and absolute discharge for both sexes. All rows do not add to 100% due to rounding of percentages.

Source: Scottish Office 1995.

Largely, patterns repeat themselves. Young women are treated more leniently at the lower end of the sentence tariff, with even more leniency when they are charged with either simple assault or shoplifting as their main charge. While still treated more leniently, young women and young men receive more similar penalties when the main charge proven is 'other theft'. One other exception to the typical pattern is the decreased use of fines for young women whose main charge is breach of the peace or simple assault.

More sophisticated statistical techniques and case information might be able to explain the greater leniency with which young women as a group are sentenced in Scotland, in non-chivalrous, legal terms. From the statistical information readily available from the Scottish Office, however, the Scottish data on young offenders do not appear to replicate Farrington and Morris's ground-breaking study of a Cambridge Magistrate Court (1983), where differences were explained away by legal criteria. When sentencing is controlled for type of offence and partially controlled for record, evidence of greater leniency in the overall sentencing of girls and young women remains.

Offending and deviance

Is leniency reserved for those women who commit stereotypically 'feminine' offences? Thus, offences that girls and young women were most likely to commit, taking up the majority of their offences, were used for comparisons with similar offending by boys and young men. This section will seek to consider leniency by type of offence, to consider women who are 'triply deviant' – not only do they go against societal rules and stereotypes of a 'feminine role' by offending, but they also commit offences that are not stereotypically 'feminine'.

Stereotypically 'feminine' and 'masculine' crimes

Certain literature identifies particular crimes as 'feminine' and others as 'masculine'. Prostitution, embezzlement and fraud, and shoplifting are commonly identified as 'feminine' crimes, whereas violent crimes such as murder, robbery, use of dangerous weapons and fire-raising, vandalism and, to a lesser extent, white-collar crimes are typically considered 'masculine' crimes (see for example, Adler 1975; Elliott 1988; Pollak 1950; Willemsen and Van Schie 1989; Williams, Winfree Jr and Theis Jr 1984). A mixture of reasons is given for these differences.

For example, Pollak identifies only prostitution as a 'specifically female' crime but that women tend to commit other crimes such as shoplifting and poisoning due to crime-promoting influences and available opportunities (1950, pp.155, 158–159). Certain writers merely rely on statistical differences to decide what crimes are most likely to be committed by men rather than women, and vice versa.

Table 6.13 Initial police reports for 15-year-olds, whose main charges are shoplifting, fraud, serious assault and robbery (Scotland 1989)

	Per cent (%)		
All actions	*Warning*	*Referral to Reporter*	*Referral to Procurator Fiscal*
Shoplifting			
Boys (100%) (N=651)	12	71	17
Girls (100%) (N=249)	16	64	20
Fraud			
Boys (100%) (N=32)	6	84	9
Girls (100%) (N=16)	31	50	19
Serious Assault			
Boys (100%) (N=152)	<0	59	41
Girls (100%) (N=24)	8	46	46
Robbery			
Boys (100%) (N=69)	1	62	36
Girls (100%) (N=3)	–	33	67

Note: All rows do not add to 100% due to rounding of percentages.
Source: Scottish Office 1995.

According to the theory behind 'triply deviancy', women will be treated more harshly than men if they commit 'masculine' crimes. Statistics are considered in Table 6.13 for children and young people committing shoplifting and fraud ('feminine' crimes) and serious assault and robbery ('masculine' crimes), as tests for these theories.

The stereotypes about 'feminine' and 'masculine' crimes appear true for shoplifting, but not for serious assault. Shoplifting was a much larger proportion of girls' main charges (23%) than boys' (7%). While serious assault, robbery, and fraud were each a very small percentage of either boys' or girls' main charges, serious assault shared a similar percentage of both boys' or girls' main charges. In terms of police action, rather than being treated more leniently for the stereotypically 'feminine' crimes of shoplifting or fraud, if anything young women were treated more harshly. When committing stereotypically 'masculine' crimes such as serious assault they were treated slightly more harshly than boys for assault, and considerably more harshly for robbery. However, only three girls had robbery as their main charge.

As a proportion of their main charges proved, young women were more likely than young men to commit shoplifting or fraud (although fraud charges were small for both sexes) (see Table 6.14). Young women did tend to be treated more leniently at both ends of the sentencing tariff, with the exception of equal referrals to Community Service Orders for shoplifting. Very few young women committed robbery or serious assault for their main charges, whereas such crimes were both 1 per cent of young men's total main charges proved. While comparisons are thus somewhat suspect, young women continue to be treated more leniently at both ends of the sentencing tariff. The one substantive difference is the increased use of the 'welfare' option of probation for young women compared to men when their main charge is either robbery or serious assault. This could suggest that, rather than being treated more harshly, the protectionism of the 'chivalry' factor comes into operation for young women committing stereotypically 'masculine' crimes.

These statistics provide some numerical support for a division between 'masculine' and 'feminine' crimes. But rather than being treated more harshly when young women commit stereotypically 'masculine' crimes, the courts appear to be more protective towards young women than to young men, with a higher use of probation for young women.

Severity of response

Another way to consider responses by the criminal justice system to 'triply deviant' girls and young women is to approach the issue from the opposite direction: what charges result in the most severe action by the criminal justice system? Are the crimes and offences typically considered 'masculine'?

Table 6.14 Penalties for young people (aged 16–20 years) whose main charges proved are shoplifting, fraud, serious assault and robbery (Scotland 1993)

	Per cent (%)					
All penalties Main charge	*Other1*	*Admonishment/ caution*	*Fine*	*Probation*	*Community Service Order (CSO)*	*Custody*
Shoplifting						
Males (100%) (N=1173)	1	18	53	9	3	16
Females (100%) (N=583)	1	33	47	9	3	6
Fraud						
Males (100%) (N=235)	3	11	74	4	3	5
Females (100%) (N=98)	9	14	69	4	1	2
Serious assault						
Males (100%) (N=381)	3	7	21	10	13	46
Females (100%) (N=11)	–	18	9	36	9	27
Robbery						
Males (100%) (N=309)	3	4	10	13	11	58
Females (100%) (N=6)	–	83	–	17	–	–

Note:

1 'Other' includes compensation orders and absolute discharge for both sexes. All rows do not add to 100% due to rounding of percentages.

Source: Scottish Office 1995.

Children

From the data that are available, types of offences can be arranged into rank order according to the severity of action that they elicit, keeping age constant. For example, the offences for which police action is taken against 15-year-old girls can be ranked according to which are most likely to be referred by the police to the Procurator Fiscal. In 1989, over 50 per cent of 15-year-old girls committing these offences were referred to the Procurator Fiscal: 'other' motor vehicle; robbery; serious assault, unlawful use of vehicle, theft of motor vehicle, theft by opening lockfast places and drugs (Scottish Office 1995). Boys as a group were treated more leniently for all of these offences, and considerably more leniently for five of them. For the six highest ranked offences, the behaviour can be seen as running counter to traditional role expectations. In particular, both robbery and serious assault are typically considered 'masculine' crimes by the literature. Could this explain the harsher treatment for the girls?

The actual number of girls involved in these offences is small. There were only eight cases of police action against 15-year-old girls on serious assault and only two cases of robbery. Though these numbers are too small for definitive statistical claims, aggregating data over several years might be. It can be suggested, however, that girls could be perceived by the police as deviant: not only against the law and against traditional gendered roles, but also because of their actual numbers.

Young adults

Analysis can be undertaken in terms of sentencing, for 16–20-year-olds, taking custody, Community Service Orders and probation as the more serious penalties. The offences for which 16–20-year-old women are most likely to receive one of these three penalties are shown in Table 6.15.

The data do not substantially demonstrate the potential impact of 'triple deviancy', if the two young women who committed fire-raising are excluded because of their minuscule numbers. Young women are treated somewhat more severely for serious assault and handling offensive weapons, which could be seen as stereotypically 'masculine' crimes. Yet they are treated more leniently than men for housebreaking. The data do not illuminate the actual gravity of the offence, to see if the women are receiving penalties higher up (or in the case of assault, lower on) the tariff for similar offences.

Table 6.15 Young adults (16–20 years old) receiving custody, Community Service Orders or probation, by main charges women are most likely to receive these penalties for (Scotland 1993)

	Custody, Community Service Order or Probation			
	Number		*Per cent (%)*	
	Young women	*Young men*	*Young women*	*Young men*
Fire-raising	2	50	100	48
Serious assault	28	381	72	69
Handling offensive weapons	12	677	58	44
Housebreaking	54	2302	57	65

Source: Scottish Office 1995.

Worrall (1987) argues that probation is used in England and Wales as if it was lower down the sentencing tariff for women, than for men. Further, probation can be considered a 'welfare' option (Webb 1984). Indeed, for all the main charges in Table 6.15, young women are more likely to receive probation than custody or a Community Service Order, while men are consistently more likely to receive custody than the other two options. If custody alone is taken to be indicative of response severity, then the likelihood of women receiving harsher penalties than men appears to be diminished (Table 6.16).

Table 6.16 Young adults (16–20 years old) receiving custody, by the four main charges young women are most likely to receive custody for (Scotland 1993)

	Custody, Community Service Order or Probation			
	Number		*Per cent (%)*	
	Young women	*Young men*	*Young women*	*Young men*
Serious assault	11	174	27	69
Homicide	28	31	18	100
Housebreaking	54	785	17	34
Theft by opening lockfast places	22	317	14	20

Source: Scottish Office 1995.

At first appearance, then, young women do not seem to be receiving custodial sentences for offences at the same rate as men, even for offences that appear to run contrary to conventional gender roles. On the other hand, the statistical sources available give little indication as to the seriousness of the offences with the offence type, for which women and men are given custodial sentences, nor their previous offending behaviour.

In summary, girls but not young women appear affected by 'triple deviancy', where they receive harsher action for 'masculine' crimes than when boys commit them.[7] Young women appear to treated more protectively, by receiving probation rather than custody, on the higher end the sentencing tariff.

Offending and background

Recent research repeatedly suggests that leniency or chivalry only extends to certain categories of women: race, class and marital status being categories around which the leniency of disposals may vary. Neither *Criminal Proceedings in Scottish Courts* nor *Prison Statistics Scotland* provides information on these variables. Some data, however, can be found in *The Community Service Bulletin,* in regards to community service places given in 1991. As explained above, Community Service is the most important alternative to imprisonment, and considered the highest non-custodial disposal on the sentencing tariff.

Table 6.17 Offenders given Community Service, by marital status (Scotland 1991)

	Number		*Per cent (%)*	
	Female	*Male*	*Female*	*Male*
Single	166	3208	49	68
Married	102	1171	30	25
Widowed, Divorced or Separated	71	308	21	7
Total	339	4687	100	100

Source: Scottish Office 1994a, Table 7.

7 Noting, however, the limits of the statistics available and the constraints on police as indicated by footnote 6.

Over two-thirds of all men given Community Service in 1990 were single compared with less than half of all women (Table 6.17). Over 30 per cent of all women were married and 51 per cent had been married at some point, compared with only 32 per cent of all men. The higher proportion of married or once married women given Community Service cannot be explained away by the tendency for Community Service to be given to younger people and for women to marry earlier than men. Women referred to Community Service tend to be considerably older than men, as the numbers in Table 6.18 indicate.

Table 6.18 Offenders referred for Community Service[1] after referral, by age and sex (Scotland 1991)

	Number		*Per cent (%)*	
Age (years)	*Females*	*Males*	*Females*	*Males*
16–17	27	662	8	14
18–20	44	1458	13	31
21–25	89	1214	26	26
26–30	71	624	21	13
31–40	80	499	23	11
41+	30	254	9	5
Total	**341**	**4711**	**100**	**100**

Note:
1 Includes Community Service Orders given with probation.
Source: Scottish Office 1994a, Table 4A.

While only at the level of conjecture, questions about the influence of marital status and age on community service referrals can be asked. Are older women preferred because they tend to be married, or are married women preferred because they tend to be older? Making assumptions by taking the two tables together, are older married women preferred over younger single women for Community Service? Are younger single women less likely to be held responsible for their actions and therefore considered less appropriate for community service?

Without further information on legal criteria and data connecting marital status, gender and age, no answers can be given definitely. What the statistics do show is that only older women (31–40 and 41+

years) were as likely to receive community service as custody in 1991; for all other age groups, custody was more likely (Scottish Office 1994a, Table 6B).

Conclusions

As so often with analysis of statistics gathered for other purposes, official Scottish statistics provide some tantalising half-answers to some of the questions posed by this chapter. Official criminality is largely a male pastime, although women are gradually increasing their official involvement in the Scottish criminal justice system. Whether this represents an actual increase in female law-breaking in general, an increase in particular types of law-breaking, or an increase in detection and action by the criminal justice system are questions unanswerable by official statistics. Certainly, the greater official increase occurs in offences, rather than crimes, with a mix of stereotypically 'feminine' and 'masculine' offences on the increase. But even while this pattern is evident, the insignificance of female crime must be kept in mind: only 16 per cent of all charges proved were against women.

The statistics also suggest we should challenge any proposition that men offend as part of 'growing up' but women offend because they are 'abnormal' or 'immoral'. Female offending is not constant throughout women's lives, but peaks when women are 18 years old as does offending with men.

Both girls under 15 and young women between the ages of 16 and 20 tend to be treated, on aggregate, more leniently both when initial police reports are made, and at both ends of the sentencing tariff: girls and young women are more likely to receive formal warnings, admonishments, cautions or discharges than boys and young men, and are less likely to be sentenced to custody. Girls and young women are less likely to receive Community Service Orders than boys and young men, but appear to have drawn equal in very recent years in sentences of fines and probation. The greater leniency at both ends of the tariff could co-exist with greater protectionism to girls and young women. More girls and young women could be drawn into the net of the criminal justice system, for offences that would not attract the attention of the criminal justice system if they were done by boys and young men.

Even when attempts are made to control initial police action by type of offence and criminal record, amongst girls to which the the patterns largely continue. However, in the types of charges amongst girls to which the criminal justice system responds most harshly, girls at age 15 appear to be treated more severely than boys, with more severe action or sentencing being. Girls may be disadvantaged because so few of them commit crimes leading to such sentences, and/or because such crimes (like robbery and serious assault) can be considered stereotypically 'masculine' crimes. However, when girls age 15 commit the stereotypically 'feminine' crimes of shoplifting or fraud, they are treated more harshly than boys of the same age committing the same crimes. Young women (age 16–20) appear to be treated more leniently for 'feminine' crimes. When they are sentenced for the stereotypically 'masculine' crimes of robbery or serious assault, however, they are not treated more harshly but are more likely to receive probation than men. The general presumption of greater leniency towards girls and young women appears too simplistic. Evidence suggests that at times the system can be more protective or hasher to girls and young women, depending on particular types of offences and the age of the offender. While patterns generally continue when attempts are made to control for legal variables, the aberrations for these patterns for particular offences demonstrate vividly the need for further information. The aberrations indeed may be erased if the full content of the legal variables was known and controlled for; on the other hand, the aberrations may throw into question some of the patterns presumed to be thrown up by the 'chivalry factor'.

Statistics from the *Community Service Bulletin* provide one of the few opportunities in the official statistics to consider other factors besides gender in female sentencing: that is, marital status and thus the influence of 'domesticity' ideologies. While certainly Samuel 1994 reports on the dearth of community resources for women serving such orders, such reasons do not fully explain why being, or having been, married appears to increase the granting of CSOs for women but not for men. Once again, controlling for criminal record, type of offence, severity of offence and other background characteristics would be needed before the impact of domestic arrangements on sentencing could be assessed.

Given the findings of Carlen (1987), the effect of perceived parental control on girls and young women on decisions by the criminal justice system requires investigation. Carlen found, in her largely qualitative research on young working class women in and leaving residential care, that they were perceived as 'out of control' by the criminal justice system because they lacked a parental home and its control. Thus, just as older women who do not appear controlled by their domestic situation, the younger women were subject to harsher treatment from the system. Whether young women from or leaving residential care are similarly 'at risk' from the criminal justice system is unanswered by the official Scottish statistics.

Official statistics do not demonstrate what ideological factors influence action taken by the criminal justice system against women. The data do, however, demonstrate some of the combinations of leniency and harshness that are attributed to the 'chivalry factor' in the literature on female offending. Considerably more detailed statistics and qualitative research are required to identify accurately why girls and young women appear to have different interactions with the criminal justice system than boys and young men. Such investigations must consider the social context of both the young people and the criminal justice system: for example, the potential influence of parental control, racial discrimination, class discrimination, and available resources. What this initial exploration does demonstrate is the need for just such further investigations; the new requirement in the Criminal Justice (Scotland) Act 1995 to publish information in relation to offenders' race and sex will be a valuable addition to our knowledge.

References

Adler, F. (1975) *Sisters in Crime*. New York: McGraw-Hill.

Asquith, S., Buist, M., Macauley, C., Montgomery, M. and Loughran, N. (1995) Children, young people and offending in Scotland: a research review. Unpublished report for the Scottish Office. Glasgow: Centre for the Study of the Child and Society, University of Glasgow.

Austin, R.L. (1993) Recent trends in official male and female crime rates: the convergence controversy. *Journal of Criminal Justice 21*, 5, 447–466.

Campbell, A. (1981) *Girl Delinquents*. Oxford: Basil Blackwell.

Campbell, A. (1991) *The Girls in the Gang*. 2nd ed. Oxford: Blackwell Publishers.

Carlen, P. (1987) Out of care, into custody: dimensions and deconstructions of the state's regulation of twenty-two young working-class women. In P. Carlen and A. Worrall (eds) *Gender, Crime and Justice*. Milton Keynes: Open University Press.

Carlen, P. and Worrall, A. (1987) Introduction: gender, crime and justice. In P. Carlen and A. Worrall (eds) *Gender, Crime and Justice.* Milton Keynes: Open University Press.

Chesney-Lind, M. (1988) Girls in jail. *Crime and Delinquency 34,* 2, 150–168.

Chesney-Lind, M. (1993) Girls, gangs and violence: anatomy of a backlash. *Humanity and Society 17,* 3, 321–344.

Children in Scotland (1995) *Scotland's Family Factsheet,* prepared by E.K.M. Tisdall with E. Donaghie. Edinburgh: HMSO.

Eaton, M. (1986) *Justice for Women? Family, Court and Social Control.* Milton Keynes: Open University Press.

Eaton, M. (1987) The question of bail: magistrates' responses to applications for bail on behalf of men and women defendants. In P. Carlen and A. Worrall (eds) *Gender, Crime and Justice.* Milton Keynes: Open University Press.

Edwards, A.R. (1989) Sex/gender, sexism and criminal justice: some theoretical considerations. *International Journal of the Sociology of Law 17,* 165–184.

Eisenman, R. and Kritsonis, W. (1993) Race, sex, and age: a nationwide study of juvenile crime. *Psychology 30,* 3/4, 66–68.

Elliott, D. (1988) *Gender, Delinquency and Society: A Comparative Study of Male and Female Offenders and Juvenile Justice in Britain.* Aldershot: Avebury.

Farrington, D. and Morris, A. (1983) Sex, sentencing and conviction. *Journal of Criminology 23,* 3, 229–248.

Genders, E. and Player, E. (1986) Women's imprisonment: the effects of youth custody. *British Journal of Criminology 26,* 4, 357–371.

Heidensohn, F. (1987) Women and crime: questions for criminology. In P. Carlen and A. Worrall (eds) *Gender, Crime and Justice.* Milton Keynes: Open University Press.

Lombroso, C. and Ferrero, W. (1895) *The Female Offender.* With an introduction by W.D. Morrison. London: T. Fisher Unwin.

Nagel, S.S. and Weitzman, L.J. (1971) Women as litigants. *The Hastings Law Journal 23,* 1, 171–98.

Petrie, C. (1986) *The Nowhere Girls.* Aldershot: Gower.

Pollak, O. (1950) *The Criminality of Women.* Philadelphia: University of Pennsylvania Press.

Samuel, E. (1994) Criminal justice and related services for young adult offenders: gender issues. In S. Asquith and E. Samuel *Criminal Justice and Related Services for Young Adult Offenders: A Review.* Edinburgh: HMSO.

Scottish Office (1991a) *Children and Crime, Scotland 1989*. Statistical Bulletin, Criminal Justice Series, CRJ/1991/3, October. Edinburgh: HMSO.

Scottish Office (1991b) *Criminal Proceedings in Scottish Courts, 1989*. Statistical Bulletin, Criminal Justice Series, CRJ/1991/5, December. Edinburgh: HMSO.

Scottish Office (1992) *Criminal Proceedings in Scottish Courts, 1991*. Statistical Bulletin, Criminal Justice Series, CRJ/1992/6, October. Edinburgh: HMSO.

Scottish Office (1993) *Criminal Proceedings in Scottish Courts, 1992*. Statistical Bulletin, Criminal Justice Series, CRJ/1993/8, November. Edinburgh: HMSO.

Scottish Office (1994a) *Community Service Bulletin, 1991*. Statistical Bulletin, Social Work Series, SWK/CS/1994/10, June. Edinburgh: HMSO.

Scottish Office (1994b) *Criminal Proceedings in Scottish Courts, 1993*. Statistical Bulletin, Criminal Justice Series, CRJ/1994/6, November. Edinburgh: HMSO.

Scottish Office (1995) Private correspondence.

Shelden, R. and Chesney-Lind, M. (1993) Gender and race differences in delinquent careers. *Juvenile and Family Court Journal 44*, 3, 73–90.

Steffensmeier, D., Allan, E. and Streifel, C. (1989) Development and female crime: a cross-national test of alternative explanations. *Social Forces 68*, 1, 262–283.

Steffensmeier, D., Kramer, J. and Streifel, C. (1993) Gender and imprisonment decisions. *Criminology 31*, 3, 411–446.

Thomas, W.I. (1923) *The Unadjusted Girl*. Boston: Little, Brown and Co.

Tisdall, E.K.M. with Donnaghie, E. (1995) *Scotland's Family Factsheet*. Prepared for Children in Scotland. Edinburgh: HMSO.

Webb, D. (1984) More on gender and justice: girl offenders on supervision. *Sociology 18*, 3, 367–381.

Willemsen, T. and van Schie, E.C.M. (1989) Sex stereotypes and responses to juvenile delinquency. *Sex Roles 20*, 11/12, 623–638.

Williams, L., Winfree Jr., L.T. and Theis, Jr., H.E. (1984) Women, crimes, and judicial dispositions: a comparative examination of the female offender. *Sociological Spectrum 4*, 2/3, 249–273.

Worrall, A. (1987) Sisters in law? Women defendants and women magistrates. In P. Carlen and A. Worrall (eds) *Gender, Crime and Justice*. Milton Keynes: Open University Press.

Chapter 7

The Community Based Alternative

Intermediate Treatment for Young Offenders

Alex Robertson and Derick McClintock[1]

Those wishing to belittle the notion that intermediate treatment (I.T.) may form an effective approach to dealing with youngsters in trouble with the law have never had far to look when seeking ammunition for their cause. In an early analysis, Hinton (1974, p.239), for example, characterised intermediate treatment as: 'a somewhat vacuous phrase used to describe new forms of community treatment of children and young persons brought before the juvenile court'. Elsewhere, Adams *et al.* (1981, p.3) have remarked that: 'intermediate treatment...has proved flexible to the point where it slips between the fingers of definition', while Nellis (1989, p.173) argues that ambiguity over the aims and methods of I.T. had by the mid-1980s become 'an impediment to good public relations', with the result that: 'a number of areas abandoned it, without there being any clear consensus as to what it should be replaced with'. Ames (1991, p.2) has more recently and more charitably reasoned that, as in other areas of social-work practice, the shifts and ambiguities of I.T. 'reflect a complex interlacing of existing legislation, political judgments and practice "knowledge"'.

The term intermediate treatment is itself redolent of ambiguity. The description *intermediate* implies interventions lying somewhere between traditional, one-to-one supervision, and full-time residential care requiring removal from the home. In terms of social-work theory, it draws on notions of constructive activity and participation in the community (Home Office 1968). The word *treatment* to some degree

---

1 Professor McClintock, who co-directed a research project with Dr Robertson funded by the Social Work Services Group on Intermediate Treatment in Scotland, died in May 1994. This chapter is affectionately dedicated to his memory.

connotes an intervention along the lines of the medical model, as developed in the heyday of the rehabilitation ideology. Some have suggested that in contemporary society, where the rehabilitation model is no longer accepted as the basis of intervention in dealing with children in trouble, the term I.T. should be abandoned. In Scotland, following the philosophy developed in the report of the Kilbrandon Committee (1964), 'child care' and 'social education' are perhaps more appropriate descriptions of interventions designed to assist children in trouble. The considerable discussion and literature on the term intermediate treatment is not of mere semantic interest. It lies at the centre of the whole controversy over the appropriateness of different approaches to dealing with youngsters in difficulty.

The development of I.T.

I.T. is generally viewed as a form of social work, although it has also been referred to as primarily social education or child care. The term 'intermediate treatment' was first used in a recommendation contained in the White Paper *Children in Trouble* (Home Office 1968), which set out government proposals for changes in legal procedures for dealing with juvenile offenders in England and Wales. The White Paper proposed I.T. should become a statutory option available to magistrates in juvenile courts and be a statutory responsibility of social services departments. It was established in England and Wales by the Children and Young Persons Act 1969, as an intermediate measure between home care and custody (Leissner, Powley and Evans 1977, p.16).

Jones (1985, pp.iii–iv) argues that the move towards I.T. during the 1960s developed mainly out of growing dissatisfaction with traditional methods of dealing with children in trouble. Young people appearing before juvenile courts at this time were either committed to residential care, or placed under supervision by a social worker. There was concern over on the one hand the cost and apparent ineffectiveness of residential training (see, for example, Tutt 1974); and on the other, the inappropriateness of a method which removed children from their peer groups and relied on the 'artificial' setting of an office interview to effect changes in their behaviour (Davies 1969).

There was in addition a growing concern with the quality of life experienced by youngsters living in deprived circumstances, and an attempt to compensate for the disadvantages of poor urban environments through positive discrimination and community development (Adams *et al.* 1981, chs.1–2). Various theories of delinquency suggested that the root causes of the problem lay within the social environment of the child, and emphasis began to be placed on preventive work with pre-delinquent children. Subcultural, 'drift' and social deprivation theories suggested that the way to reduce delinquency would be to offer new opportunities, in order to redirect young people's energies into creative and socially acceptable pursuits (Cohen 1955; Cloward and Ohlin 1961; Downes 1966). The child was 'seen as deprived and as a victim of the social environment rather than as a destroyer of it' (Jones and Kerslake 1979, p.2).

Additional support for a more benign approach came from labelling theory (Adams *et al.* 1981, pp.14–15). Arguing that 'deviance' is more a function of the way people respond to particular behaviours than an inherent feature of the behaviours themselves, labelling theorists suggest that by over-reacting to 'deviant' actions we may actually reinforce the offender's deviant identity and increase the likelihood of his reoffending (Becker 1963; Lemert 1972). In order to avoid this, an alternative to institutional care should be introduced as part of a more comprehensive service to young offenders in the community. (See also Rutherford 1986.)

Complementary to these developments, social work theory and practice had also begun to be influenced by a groupwork emphasis. Following the development of social groupwork techniques, mainly in the United States, many people 'believed that a primary cause of juvenile delinquency was peer group pressure, and that groupwork could actively convert these pressures into a constructive force for change' (Jones 1985, p.3.). Groups were seen as both a diagnostic and a therapeutic tool. Young people's 'true' behaviour patterns would manifest themselves more readily in groups; and problems thus be exposed for analysis and redirection as they actually occurred. It was held that this could best be done in small groups with a high staff ratio.

I.T. in England and Wales

Initially used to refer to a wide range of provisions for youngsters in trouble or at risk, I.T. had by the mid-1970s largely become a 'form of low-intensity preventive social work' (Lilly 1992, p.198). Henderson (1979), for example, saw I.T. programmes at this time as addressing the needs of four main categories of children, whom she specified as: disadvantaged children; those with communication difficulties; those with relationship problems; and those on the fringes of delinquency.

During the 1970s the use of custodial sentences for juvenile offenders increased steadily, while the incidence of care orders remained static. Bottoms *et al.* (1990, pp.2–3; see also Lilly 1992, pp.199–202) ascribe this to 'confusion and...inter-agency conflict in English juvenile justice' following the partial implementation by the Conservative Government of the 1969 Children and Young Persons Act. Disenchantment with a 'welfare' approach to work with juvenile offenders became widespread. The goal, foreshadowed in the 1969 Act, of replacing detention centres with I.T. was seen increasingly as an impossible dream. There was also concern that an emphasis on preventive work with children 'at risk' was drawing youngsters who had not committed offences into an ever-widening 'net' of community-based programmes which the public saw as catering for delinquents (Jones 1980). The 'net-widening' propensities of I.T. should therefore be curtailed to let it concentrate on 'true' offenders.

As a consequence of these trends, a group of academics at the University of Lancaster mounted a campaign to confine the use of I.T. to a range of high-intensity alternatives to custody and residential care (Thorpe *et al.* 1980). Arguing for a new emphasis on 'systems management', this group stressed the need to monitor and control the way young offenders were processed within the juvenile justice system, with particular emphasis on diverting the young person from the court (Lilly 1992, pp.201–202). Around the same time I.T. practitioners in many parts of the country began to evolve a new way of working, dubbed the 'new orthodoxy' by Jones (1985). This ascribed less importance to meeting needs, replacing this with a more tariff-based approach and a corresponding emphasis on programmes for more serious offenders who would normally have been sentenced to custody or residential care (Blagg and Smith 1989, pp.100–105; Bottoms *et al.* 1990, ch.2).

The Criminal Justice Act of 1982 moved the focus away from preventive work in England and Wales. At the same time, it attempted to encourage I.T.'s use as an alternative to custody. Under the 1982 Act, courts were enjoined to use custodial sentences only if 'no other method of dealing with (the offender) is appropriate'. A DHSS circular issued in the following year made money available to help local authorities develop intensive community-based programmes as alternatives to custody.

The Criminal Justice Acts of 1991 and 1993 further consolidated this movement away from custodial sentences (Wasik and Taylor 1994). The 1991 Act also renamed juvenile courts as 'youth courts' and extended the age at which individuals are regarded as young persons for criminal justice purposes from 16 to 17. One further change made by the 1982 Act was the introduction of a distinction between *discretionary* and *stipulated* I.T. Discretionary I.T. gives the supervising officer the power to require the young person to participate in specified activities. Under stipulated I.T. the programme of activities is specified by the court, rather than being left to the judgment of the supervisor (Walters 1984, pp.129–132, Lilly 1992, p.200). An I.T. order permits a juvenile to be removed from home for a maximum of 90 days. If a supervision order has been made for the maximum of three years, I.T. will usually be ordered for thirty days in a year.

I.T. in Scotland

The Scottish system for dealing with children in trouble has developed on a completely different basis. While the Social Work (Scotland) Act of 1968 permitted the development of intermediate treatment, it made no specific mention of it, nor did it place any legal requirement on local authorities to develop I.T. schemes. I.T. in Scotland has thus never been formally linked to the system of juvenile justice, nor has it formed part of any child care legislation. Instead, it has been associated with a community-based welfare approach towards dealing with young people in general. Its development has depended on individual local initiatives, with central government (normally in the shape of the Scottish Office Social Work Services Group) providing encouragement and financial help. Nor did the Act contain any compulsory requirement for the young person to attend I.T.; and although it is now within a children's hearing's powers to require attendance at, for example, a youth group, such participation is in practice achieved by voluntary means.

While Blagg and Smith (1989, p.100) are perhaps too generous in their assessment of Scottish I.T. when they suggest it possesses 'an air of optimism not always evident further south', the same authors succinctly state the main ways in which it differs from its southern counterpart:

> compared with England and Wales, [I.T. in Scotland] has retained a preventive focus; it is concerned to avoid labelling and stigma; it is broad-based and relatively diffuse in its aims and in the range of young people it deals with; it is not exclusively a social work activity but also involves community and youth workers; [and] it has always entailed a mix of statutory and voluntary activity. (p.100)

The Scottish Office initially played an active part in promoting I.T. Its Memorandum of December 1974 stressed the need to provide help in relation to the child's environment. In its general guidelines, the Scottish Office indicated that projects should focus on the needs of socially deprived and delinquent children and attempt to create a relevant set of experiences in the environment in which they lived. Intermediate treatment was to be seen as not simply a means of social control, but a way of compensating deprived children for certain social handicaps. Despite the lack of a legislative link between the hearings system and I.T., the Social Work Services Group (SWSG) also expressed the hope that I.T. schemes would form an additional care measure available to the Children's Hearings. By the end of the 1970s SWSG had however noted that despite encouragement and funding, I.T. had been slow to develop in Scotland.

In 1983, a working party report noted the piecemeal development of I.T. and emphasised the need for joint planning and evaluation of provisions. The detailed survey of I.T. carried out by Gallagher on behalf of SWSG (Jones 1985) showed the diversity of programmes that then existed in Scotland, with no joint planning at either central or regional levels. One of the drawbacks of the Scottish development of I.T. seems to have been the broad range over which programmes have evolved and the lack of precise accountability for development, which might be in part attributable to the diverse funding of programmes from central government, local authorities and the voluntary sector. By the end of the 1980s it was clear that a fundamental review of policy options was required.

The content of I.T.

A considerable number of I.T. projects have published statements of their aims and general approach and these testify to the great diversity of philosophy and methods tried out in this field (see, for example, Newsam 1983; Wood 1983; Stone 1984; Farrell 1985; Jones 1985, pp.12–16; Skinner 1985, section E; Blickem 1986). Some order has been imposed on this apparent chaos by three surveys in particular. These clearly highlight the differences in the philosophy underlying I.T. on the two sides of the border, while reflecting also workers' attempts to reconcile welfare and judicial goals.

In a useful discussion paper, Downie and Ames (1986) identify five main models of I.T. The *treatment* model construes troublesome behaviour as a symptom of some underlying malady, which I.T. seeks to treat. The *containment* model focuses on the child's legal obligation to attend a programme for a stated period, using supervision requirements to set controls upon the child's behaviour to reduce his delinquency. The *occupation* model sees its main task as offering adventurous activities to bored teenagers, to compensate for the disadvantages of deprivation and so stresses the need for leisure activities and opportunities to develop healthy relations. Like the occupation model, the *youth club* model sees the problem as one of confronting disadvantage; but aims to provide enriching experiences for all young people, not only for young offenders or children 'at risk'. The *community work* model also sees problems as caused by elements in the social environment and seeks to tackle these at root. It stresses the need for any programme to be 'relevant' to the child. Relatively small local clubs are thus seen as preferable to lavishly equipped youth centres some distance from the child's home.

In her report to the Intermediate Treatment Resource Centre (ITRC), Helen Jones presented information from a survey of 76 I.T. initiatives in Scotland in the early 1980s (Jones 1985, pp.6–7; Intermediate Treatment Resource Centre 1986). She found it was quite common for schemes to change considerably in their aims and/or methods after they had been in existence for one or two years, only a small number of schemes having existed for more than five years. This obviously indicates a degree of flux in I.T. provision.

Jones proposed the following indicators, in order of importance, for the classification of I.T. schemes:

1. the intensity of I.T. provision in groups: a measure of both the frequency with which the group met and the type of work carried out within it. Five levels of intensity were identified:
   - after-school 'open' youth club facility
   - one evening per week activity session
   - one evening per week task-oriented groupwork session
   - two or more evenings per week task-oriented groupwork
   - daily school work;
2. the proportion of children under supervision requirements
3. the staffing arrangements in relation to the number of children accommodated.

Using varying combinations of these indicators, the following classification of I.T. schemes was constructed:

> *high intensity I.T. schemes* providing frequent task-oriented groupwork sessions or schooling, with a very high proportion of children under supervision and a very high ratio of staff to children;
>
> *medium intensity I.T. schemes* providing once or twice weekly task-oriented groupwork sessions, with a lower proportion of children under supervision and a lower ratio of staff to children than in the high intensity schemes;
>
> *low intensity I.T. schemes* providing youth club facilities or once-weekly activity sessions, with only a few children under supervision and large numbers of children in relation to the number of staff.

The *high intensity* category also has the most structured programmes. Groups meet every day (often providing alternative schooling) according to a pre-arranged programme. Children at this end of the continuum are often in danger of removal into residential care. High-intensity I.T. schemes can also be used to support a young person on his/her return from residential care back into the community.

In Scotland 'heavy end' groups of this kind require attendance either all day (during school term time) or on four evenings every week. Typically, the clients have been heavily involved in offending; have family (and sometimes school) problems; and are deemed in need of some kind of confidence-building experience, with group discussions forming a major part of the timetable. For this reason groups are fairly small, with a maximum of ten young people attending at any one time. Attendance at an intensive programme may be offered as an alternative to residential placement in cases where the young person and parent(s) want to remain together and residential care offers no positive safeguard of the child's or community's interests. Jones (1985, p.43) noted that very few I.T. schemes were at the 'heavy end' of I.T. provision. District or regional provision in I.T. has typically grown from community-based facilities, initially funded by outside grants (for example, Urban Aid) to more 'heavy end' facilities (McClintock *et al.* 1990).

Medium intensity schemes meet once or twice a week for task-oriented groupwork sessions, with a lower proportion of children under a supervision requirement than in high-intensity programmes. Such schemes (often called 'supervision groups') form the single most common type of provision, comprising three-fifths of all I.T. groups in Scotland (Jones 1985, p.38). The young people in such schemes are usually seen as not at imminent risk of residential care, but in need of some group experience. Clients will typically have either been involved in offending, or have family and/or school problems. All members of the medium-intensity schemes included in the Edinburgh University study (McClintock *et al.* 1990) were attending on a voluntary basis; although in this context, 'voluntary' could well mean the alternative would be admission to residential care.

Medium intensity schemes normally run once or twice a week in the afternoon after school hours, or in the early evening. Groups consist of five to ten members and usually two staff members, who may be I.T. workers or social workers with an interest in groupwork. Group sessions themselves are fairly structured in their use of time.

Low intensity schemes are the least structured of the three. This is by far the largest form of provision in terms of the numbers of youngsters involved. Certain schemes come close to youth clubs; others may be once-weekly sessions, with few children under a supervision requirement. More common names for the latter kind of schemes are 'community schemes' or 'diversionary work'.

Low intensity schemes tend to emphasise the importance of the relationship between the project and the community, aiming to prevent over-labelling of difficult young people. Referrals to such schemes are made by social workers or schools, or by the children themselves simply 'turning up'. Delinquency is not a precondition of referral. Data from the Edinburgh study suggest groups of this type generally have longer weekly sessions (two to four hours per week) than their medium intensity counterparts, although the additional time seems to be used mainly for 'free time' or 'informal activities'.

The most recent survey – by Bottoms *et al.* (1990, pp.11–23) – provides a five-fold typology of I.T. policy and practice in 94 social services departments in England and Wales during the mid-1980s.

> The *Prevention Pure* model is predominantly needs-based, with a welfare/treatment ethos and little interest in the client's status vis-à-vis the juvenile system. It gives no priority to need for systems intervention or the possible adverse effects of 'net-widening' and is not seriously interested in providing an alternative to custody or residential care. Only one area studied by Bottoms *et al.* conformed to the 'prevention pure' approach.
>
> *Prevention Plus* is concerned with meeting needs within a welfare/treatment ethos. However, it is also significantly more interested than the prevention pure model in links with the juvenile-justice system and/or alternatives to custody and care. Bottoms *et al.* see this as attempting to reconcile alternatives to custody and care with an essentially preventive policy. Twelve departments fitted into this category, offering needs-based work with a variety of young people, some of whom might be serious offenders.
>
> In the *Alternatives to Custody and Care Pure* model, I.T. is seen as exclusively for those at serious risk of custody or residential care. In most cases I.T. is perceived as for offenders only; but in a few areas is also available for non-offenders at risk of becoming subjects of care orders. Programmes offered tend to focus on offences, not needs. Twenty-two SSDs conformed to this model. Such authorities may undertake preventive work with non-offenders but this is *never* called I.T.
>
> The *Alternative to Custody and Care Plus* model bears many similarities to this last category, particularly in its primary emphasis on I.T. as an alternative to custody or care. I.T. is, however, also seen as appropriate for a 'medium range' of offenders appearing

in a juvenile court, and also occasionally for non-offenders involved in care proceedings. As in category 3, preventive work may not be undertaken as part of an I.T. programme. Twenty-seven areas corresponded to this model.

Although categories 3 and 4 between them accounted for over half of all SSDs, the largest single category (32 departments) was *Broad-Based*. This category contains at least two key elements:

- recognition of the importance of targeted I.T. provision, aiming to provide an alternative to custody or care. Such provision, however, is seen as important in itself and not subsumed within a preventive philosophy, as in 'prevention plus'
- retention of previous work with non-offenders, children 'at risk', etc., as part of the I.T. remit.

The combination of these two elements makes the broad-based category distinctive and different from both 'preventive' and 'alternatives to custody or care' policies.

With regard to the units within which I.T. was itself provided, Bottoms *et al.* identified eight basic types: (1) 'heavy end' offending only; (2) mixed, including heavy end but not preventive I.T.; (3) mixed, including heavy end *and* preventive I.T.; (4) preventive I.T. only; (5) mixed, including preventive I.T. but not heavy end or medium range; (6) mixed, including preventive I.T. and medium range but not heavy end; (7) medium range only; and (8) other types, but not including heavy end or preventive I.T. Thirteen per cent of units specialised in work at the 'heavy end'; 11 per cent in preventive activities; and 9 per cent in 'medium range' work. The remainder performed mixed functions. Overall, 46 per cent of units offered services to a mixture of offenders and non-offenders.

These emphases also had a significant bearing on the types of activity available within a programme. Discussions and practical activities were for instance more likely to feature in units of type 4–6; while social-skills education, individual work, a focus on offending behaviour, basic education and (to a lesser extent) community leisure activities were found more frequently in type 1 (heavy end) units (Bottoms *et al.* 1990, pp.122–123).

Asked what they considered to be the most important aims and objectives of their unit, 47 per cent of project directors specified improved personal functioning; 30 per cent, reduction in criminal behaviour or a change in attitude towards offending; 25 per cent, developing constructive use of leisure; 25 per cent, improving social and practical skills; and 21 per cent, providing an alternative to care and custody. Again, there was a significant relationship between the unit types and the aims identified as most important to their work (p.119).

The effectiveness of I.T.

Following an examination of research on I.T., Jones (1981) concluded that prejudices had been more influential than evidence in determining social policy towards young people in trouble. Consistent with Jones's conclusion, and in contrast to the relatively large amounts of money spent on developing individual programmes, there is something of a dearth of evidence concerning IT's effectiveness. Moreover, most of the research that is available consists of small-scale evaluations of single projects, from which it would be rash to draw definitive conclusions.

This is not the place for a lengthy analysis of the problem of identifying criteria for 'success' in dealing with juveniles. Those interested in the more detailed arguments are directed to the review by Asquith and Samuel (1994, ch.2; see also Ames 1991, pp.26–32). Suffice it to say that reoffending/recidivism is by itself an inadequate measure. Apart from such factors as individuals' skill in evading detection and variations in policing, which render re-conviction an unreliable indicator, other elements need to be borne in mind when assessing youngsters' response. Thus, the extent to which facilities prevent unnecessary readmissions to care; enhance individuals' social skills; compensate for wider deprivations; foster personal growth; or encourage constructive leisure pursuits are all equally valid considerations when intervening in youngsters' lives. Farrell (1985, p.8) makes the point well:

> To maximise the use of resources, I.T. must not only endeavour to spare young people the rigours of a custodial experience but also prepare them to deal with what may be a life-time experience of restricted choices over employment, housing and recreation.

Also relevant is the well-documented tendency for young people to 'grow out of' offending (Rutherford 1986).

Diversion from the penal system

Looking first at the ability of I.T. to prevent youngsters from coming into further contact with penal agencies, the NACRO reviews of the DHSS Intermediate Treatment Initiative (NACRO 1989a, 1989b, 1991) show a substantial reduction in the use of custody and care orders for juvenile offenders in Initiative areas. Surveying developments to 1989 NACRO (1989b, p.20; see also Allen 1991) concluded that 'Initiative projects have...contributed to the further marginalisation of the role of custody in the juvenile criminal justice system.'

In the Cambridge University survey of intensive community supervision for young offenders, Bottoms (1995) also found those sent to 'Heavy End' I.T. (HEIT) to be persistent offenders at genuine risk of a custodial sentence. NACRO (1989b, pp.18–19) did, however, note considerable variations in the use of custody between regions; and Bottoms (1995, p.32) found 'no automatic...relationship between the development of a strong HEIT programme and the reduction of custodial sentencing levels'.

More local surveys suggest I.T. can significantly reduce the use of custody. Assessing progress after the first four years of the Junction Project, Farrell (1985, p.17) points to a consistent decline in the use of custodial and care orders in the London borough where the project was operating. With regard to fears of 'net-widening', Ames (1991, p.162) found no direct evidence of courts passing more severe sentences on children attending the projects in her investigation. Nor was there evidence of civil liberties abuses, although staff commented that grounds for referral were not always clearly specified.

Recidivism rates

Denne (1983; Denne and Peel 1983) compared recidivism rates in a group of youngsters in intensive I.T. with those for a group placed in community homes. The findings suggest I.T. was more effective in reducing reoffending. Farrell (1985, p.19) looked at reconviction rates among 84 youngsters who had formed twelve separate intakes at the Junction Project. He found a substantial decline in the period between a year before and two years after the start of their participation.

Bottoms (1995) used both official and self-reported delinquency to measure reoffending. He found no statistically significant difference between youngsters in I.T. and those attending other forms of disposal on either of these indicators.

Stafford (1984) compared 14–15-year-olds attending two Birmingham I.T. centres and children of similar age and offending history who had declined I.T. Although she found a significant decline in the number of offences committed by the I.T. group in the period during and immediately following I.T., there was no difference between the two groups in rates of reconviction or offending in the 12 months after the programme ended. With regard to admissions to custody or residential care, in both the I.T. and comparison groups 66 per cent of youngsters had residential or custodial care experience prior to the study. Twelve months later, 75 per cent of the comparison and 28.2 per cent of the I.T. group had been received into custody or care, a statistically significant difference which Stafford calculates to have yielded a saving of £3582 per young person on I.T. As against this, Knapp and Fenyo's (1995) cost-effectiveness analysis of the centres studied by Bottoms (1995) found HEIT was no more or less cost-effective than custody.

The present authors' evaluation of Scottish I.T. (McClintock *et al.* 1990) used self-report instruments to measure changes in offending behaviour among children participating in I.T. between the start of their attendance and six months later. A significant *increase* occurred over time in drug-taking among children attending I.T., but there were no other statistically significant changes. A comparison between children attending high and medium intensity I.T. and matched groups of youngsters receiving residential care or community supervision found significantly greater reductions in theft and vandalism among those undergoing more traditional forms of intervention.

An attempt was also made to gauge the extent to which I.T. performance was affected by the treatment 'climate' of the programme (Moos 1973, 1974). This showed theft tending to decline in centres which limited autonomy, involvement in the programme and expressions of anger and aggression on the part of members; in which staff were seen as less 'fair' and more controlling; and which focused on children's personal problems, rather than practical tasks. By contrast, vandalism declined where there was little emphasis on order and organisation, but a high emphasis on practical tasks. Drug-taking seemed immune to the effects of treatment climate.

On comparing the performance of the 'City' and 'Shire' HEIT projects in the Cambridge study, Bottoms (1995, pp.9–18) found significantly less official criminality among children who had attended the former centre. The City programme was community-based, concentrating on frequent 'tracking' of offenders in their local neighbourhood by an auxiliary worker working under the guidance of a centre project leader who also saw the offenders weekly. The auxiliary offered advice, guidance and training in social skills, as well as discussion of the child's offending. The Shire approach, by contrast, relied on 'packages' put together by a probation officer or social worker, comprising elements like community service, individual counselling and a befriending scheme, which could vary for different offenders. Bottoms saw the Shire approach as 'much less structured' than the City's 'tracking' project. Its results were also worse than those of the custody group. Bottoms concludes that projects which emphasise a combination of order and caring (identified as 'strong pro-social modelling') are more successful in reducing reoffending.

In a study of 102 youngsters attending I.T. in Scotland, Atkinson (1989) found reductions in clients' reported delinquent behaviour. Looking at the extent to which children and staff held congruent views of the aims of the programmes in which they were participating, this author also found staff emphasised 'treatment' (strengthening personality; developing greater self-esteem) rather than 'instrumental' or 'control' functions. Clients, by contrast, viewed I.T. in terms mainly of control and saw this as the most helpful aspect of I.T. They also attached importance to improving interpersonal (particularly family) relationships. Children proved more likely to reduce their offending if they *did not* agree with staff's objectives for I.T.

Social functioning and personal adjustment

Two of the projects in Ames's (1991) study emphasised a 'welfare' approach. This was seen as offering support to certain youngsters who would not otherwise receive help. The programmes staff thought most likely to be effective were those with clearly stated aims, a definite target group and a structured programme relevant to participants' background and experience. Bottoms (1995) found that providing an alternative to custody was the main target for most HEIT workers. Reducing reoffending was neither so strongly held nor so clearly enunciated as an aim.

In an analysis of clients' attitudes towards themselves, family, peers and authority, Atkinson (1989) found over half the children in her sample showing an improvement in their self-esteem. This was consistent with staff members' objectives for I.T., stressing as they did the importance of personal growth and improvement in clients' confidence and self-image. However, children whose perceptions of their project's aims coincided with those of staff members did no better than those of their peers who held incongruent views. Clients who thought the content of their I.T. programme to be relevant to their needs were also more likely to register improvements in self-perception and self-esteem than those who saw the programme as irrelevant. Finally, clients referred by social workers showed significantly more positive changes than those referred from other sources and Atkinson suggests this might be due to social workers' having a clearer view of I.T. than individuals in other agencies.

McClintock *et al.* 1990 found children on I.T. programmes making significant improvements in personal and social functioning, with gains in self-esteem; general self-concept; and perception of self in relation to peers. They also advanced in behaviour and performance at school; enjoyed better relationships with adults; and suffered fewer 'emotional problems'. By comparison with their counterparts in I.T., youngsters under supervision or in residential care showed greater improvement in behaviour at home and school; relations with adults; violence; and 'dominance/submission'. Bottoms (1995, pp.24–26) reports findings very similar to these from his study of English I.T. However, a comparison showed young offenders placed in custody experiencing significantly more personal problems one year after the end of treatment than those not given custodial sentences.

The present authors (McClintock *et al.* 1990) found that I.T. programmes high in clarity, identification, fairness and support produced greater improvements in self-concept, self-esteem and perception of self in relation to others. Improvements in behaviour at school were greater among children attending programmes high in staff control; and low in fairness, autonomy and expressions of anger and aggression among their participants. Attitudes to school improved most in centres high in support, clarity, satisfaction and identification with the programme; and low in autonomy, fairness and expression of anger and aggression. Children's relations with adults also benefited more in centres with high clarity, personal problem orientation, identification and satisfaction with the programme. More structured and 'intensive' programmes that involved attendance for longer average amounts of time per week also appeared to produce more positive outcomes.

'User' reactions

'User' will here be regarded as including professionals, youngsters, parents and members of the general public. In one of the earliest evaluations of I.T., Leissner *et al.* (1977) describe the development of a project based on a community-work philosophy, in which voluntary I.T. was provided as part as a range of services to the neighbourhood. They conclude that such an arrangement provided a number of potentially fruitful opportunities for working with youngsters judged to be at risk. However, 'hard core' delinquents needed extra resources and this created ill feeling among local residents.

Ames (1991) found generally positive attitudes amongst police and school staff towards the projects in her study. The police in particular welcomed the preventive focus of the centres, with which they were often closely associated, and which they saw as complementing their own crime-prevention work. Social workers commented favourably on the expertise and resources made available by the projects. There was also support for organising preventive and care-related programmes separately from those for recognised offenders. Stone (1984) notes that staff had to spend a lot of time and energy on certain referrals, which kept them away from the project for considerable periods of time. Supervising officers also felt unclear about their role in relation to the project's work.

Bottoms (1995) sought magistrates' views on I.T. While most stressed the importance of rehabilitation and had little faith in custody's ability to reduce offending, their willingness to use I.T. was also influenced by whether they saw I.T. workers as credible professionally, and felt trust in the project leader.

Robinson, Dixon and Evans (1988) conducted an evaluation of an I.T. project run as a partnership between young people, parents and social workers, with an emphasis on 'sharing power' and parental involvement in case conferences and management. The project's efforts to involve parents were 'partly designed to rebuild their confidence and to emphasise that their contribution is essential if the young person is to remain within the family' (1988, p.48). Parents saw benefits for the child and the family from their involvement in the project's work. The youngsters themselves were the ones most strongly in favour of the access to records and information-sharing that went on in the project.

According to Stone (1984) youngsters who completed the three-month programme she was studying regarded its main benefit as keeping them out of trouble. Of 28 young people, only 11 felt they had gained from individual counselling and a further 11 reported gaining nothing from groupwork. The project was, however, rated highly by these youngsters in the help it provided with personal, family and social functioning. In follow-up interviews, the unanimous view was that the project helped them think about themselves in relation to offending, but that it could achieve no more.

Both McClintock *et al.* (1990) and Bottoms (1995) found I.T. enjoying greater acceptance among parents and children. Offenders in the Cambridge study rated I.T. significantly more positively than custody or supervision orders, though HEIT attenders disliked the restrictions imposed by attendance and travel requirements. The Scottish youngsters entered I.T. with rather low expectations. Six months later, most saw themselves as having benefited from it. The main perceived gains were keeping out of trouble; help with school, family or 'general' problems; having someone to talk to who cared about them; and learning to see the consequences of their actions. The great majority also reported learning new practical skills. The most *popular* aspect of I.T. was recreational activities like sports, outings and crafts. Few aspects were actively disliked by members. A small though vociferous minority saw group discussions as reducing the value of I.T., but most seemed to value groupwork, the most *worthwhile* features of I.T. being seen as talking about problems and having contact with staff. On leaving I.T. the majority of children had found it enjoyable (68%), interesting (53%) and worthwhile (73%).

Youngsters in the comparison groups had also started with low expectations. As in the I.T. groups, these were modified by experience, similar benefits being reported to those identified by I.T. members. A considerably larger proportion of comparison-group members thought they would be able to cope with their problems when their contact with the programme ended. Like the I.T. group, increased self-confidence and greater awareness of the consequences of their actions were given as reasons for this belief. But whereas comparison-group children expressed general confidence in their own ability to cope with problems or stay out of trouble, I.T. members' confidence was less generalised, their expected ability to stay out of trouble being attributed to specific changes such as getting on better with parents, coping better at school, and having access to helpful staff. Whether this difference reflects a variation between the focus of I.T. and other forms of intervention, or to greater insight and/or realism on the part of I.T. members seems worthy of further investigation.

Bottoms (1995) found the overall degree of parental involvement in I.T. to be slight. According to the Scottish data, I.T. parents felt less involved in the programme than those of children in more traditional forms of treatment, which might be attributable to the fact that few could remember an internal review having occurred. In Scotland, both I.T. and comparison groups displayed an equally vague knowledge of what went on in the sessions their children attended, although I.T. parents were more likely to perceive an improvement in the children's behaviour in general and fewer reported their children having problems of truanting or school behaviour.

As in Bottoms's study, I.T. had greater acceptance overall among parents than conventional forms of disposal. Parents reported I.T. as more enjoyable to the children and many more saw their child as having benefited. There also seemed much greater satisfaction with I.T. among the parents themselves, possibly because of its less intrusive nature as compared with social work and child guidance. Indeed, the commonest criticism made by I.T. parents was that individual I.T. sessions should last longer and be held more frequently.

Discussion

What conclusions can be drawn from the above? It first of all seems clear that I.T. can greatly facilitate the diversion of youngsters from more severe penal measures, although the existence of I.T. projects is not *per se* sufficient to ensure this. The use of I.T. as a diversionary measure seems to depend on the degree of legitimacy accorded to the projects by those responsible for sentencing or referral decisions. The findings of both Bottoms and Ames also suggest that I.T. workers are able to combine welfare and judicial objectives in their work and that in many cases greater stress is placed on the former than the latter aims. Staff seem sensitive to the 'net-widening' potential of I.T., and such (admittedly meagre) evidence as exists suggests it need not lead to civil rights infringements.

In the case of reoffending, the data seem rather more equivocal. But accepting this fact, the evidence does on balance seem to suggest that I.T. *per se* is no more, and possibly slightly less, effective in preventing further offending than supervision, custody or residential care.

The findings of the Edinburgh research do, however, indicate that delinquency is reduced in programmes which discourage autonomy and expressions of anger and aggression and have a greater degree of structure and control by staff. Improvements in troublesome behaviour also seem to occur more readily in programmes which limit autonomy and the venting of aggression among members. These seem consistent with the indication from the Cambridge study that structured projects which emphasise order and caring are more successful in reducing recidivism. The relative failure of I.T. to reduce delinquency may to some degree be explained by projects' differing emphases. Atkinson's finding that children stressed the importance of control as opposed to a staff emphasis on treatment seems interesting in this regard.

With regard to improvements in personal and social functioning, the picture suggested by the Edinburgh results is one of programmes guided by a social work concern for personal relationships and adjustment, rather than offending, and having a fair degree of success in this regard. In the case of self concept and self-esteem, for example, improvements seem to depend on the degree of support, fairness and clarity offered by the programme; and the extent to which youngsters identify with it. In these respects, I.T. programmes seem to produce beneficial results and this may again relate to their emphasis on such elements as fairness, support and a personal problem orientation. Their lack of success in reducing delinquency does, however, also suggest that an emphasis on 'adjustment' is insufficient on its own and that an additional orientation needs to be introduced to ensure the full range of children's problems is properly addressed.

The effectiveness of I.T. might therefore be enhanced if attendance requirements were increased and structure, clarity and support more specifically integrated into the methods and philosophies of individual centres. They also indicate that children referred to I.T. are looking for a more controlled and perhaps emotionally secure environment in which the limits of tolerable behaviour are clearly defined, aggression kept under rein, and the involvement of children in running the programme restricted to a minimum.

Programme planning and internal management in I.T. should perhaps be geared to the development of more structured (though non-authoritarian) régimes. The Edinburgh findings also hint that separate approaches might, for example, be necessary on the one hand, to boost relationships and self-esteem, and on the other, to reduce disruptive behaviour; but further work is undoubtedly needed on this question. A good case could by contrast be made for the view that it is less important to concentrate on the delinquent behaviour of children who will in due course 'grow out of' offending (Rutherford 1986); that incarceration is extremely damaging to young people; and that greater long-term gains will come from attempts to improve the self-confidence, attitudes and relationship skills of individuals who may have no other opportunity for this while still living in the community.

I.T. enjoys acceptance among parents, children and professionals. This is, however, also reliant on programmes' legitimacy with these groups. Among children and parents, this possibly reflects I.T.'s less intrusive nature. From a review which suggests I.T. to be no less effective than other forms of provision, there seem to be good grounds for continuing with this least-disruptive alternative.

References

Adams, R., Allard, S., Baldwin, J. and Thomas, J. (1981) *A Measure of Diversion? Case Studies in Intermediate Treatment.* Leicester: National Youth Bureau.

Allen, R. (1991) Out of jail: the reduction in the use of penal custody for male juveniles, 1981–88. *Howard Journal of Criminal Justice 30,* 30–52.

Ames, J. (1991) *Just Deserts or Just Growing Up? Community Initiatives with Young People in Trouble.* London: National Children's Bureau.

Asquith, S. and Samuel, E. (1994) *Criminal Justice and Related Services for Young Adult Offenders: A Review.* Edinburgh: HMSO.

Atkinson, M. (1989) Clients' and Practitioners' Perceptions of Intermediate Treatment. Unpublished PhD thesis, Faculty of Social Sciences, University of Edinburgh.

Becker, H. (1963) *Outsiders: Studies in the Sociology of Deviance.* New York: Free Press.

Blagg, H. and Smith, D. (1989) *Crime, Penal Policy and Social Work.* London: Longman.

Blickem, V. (1986) *Cambridge Alternatives: A Community Initiative Designed to Provide Ways of Working with Young People.* Cambridge: Cambridge I.T.

Bottoms, A. (1995) *Intensive Community Supervision for Young Offenders: Outcomes, Process and Cost.* University of Cambridge: Institute of Criminology Publications.

Bottoms, A., Brown, P., McWilliams, B., McWilliams, W. and Nellis, M. (1990) *Intermediate Treatment and Juvenile Justice: Key Findings and*

Implications from a National Survey of Intermediate Treatment Policy and Practice. London: HMSO.

Cloward, R.A. and Ohlin, L.E. (1961) *Delinquency and Opportunity*. London: Routledge and Kegan Paul.

Cohen, A.K. (1955) *Delinquent Boys: The Culture of the Gang*. New York: Free Press.

Curtis, S. (1989) *Juvenile Offending: Prevention through Intermediate Treatment*. London: Batsford.

Davies, M. (1969) *Probationers in their Social Environment*. Home Office Research Studies, 2. London: HMSO.

Denne, J. (1983) Community care can work. *Community Care 453*, 18–21.

Denne, J. and Peel, R. (1983) Does I.T. work? *Community Care 454*, 20–21.

Downes, D.M. (1966) *The Delinquent Solution: A Study in Subcultural Theory*. London: Routledge and Kegan Paul.

Downie, J. and Ames, J. (1986) *Intermediate Treatment*. Sutton Surrey: Community Care in association with University of Sheffield Joint Unit for Social Services Research.

Farrell, M. (1985) *The Junction Project: Intensive Intermediate Treatment in Lambeth: The First Four Years*. London: Save the Children.

Gibson, B. (1989) Intermediate treatment. *Law Society Gazette 1*, 1241–1242.

Henderson, M. (1979) The opportunities and limitations of intermediate treatment. In M. Henderson and P. Bates (eds) *Intermediate Treatment: Two Papers*. Glasgow: Strathclyde Regional Council Social Work Department.

Hinton, N. (1974) Intermediate treatment. In L. Blom-Cooper (ed.) *Progress in Penal Reform*. Oxford: Clarendon Press.

Home Office (1968) *Children in Trouble*. Cm 3601. London: HMSO.

Intermediate Treatment Resource Centre (1986) *Review of I.T. in Scotland: Part 2, Regional Position Statements*. Glasgow: Scottish Intermediate Treatment Centre.

Jones, H.E. (1985) *Intermediate Treatment in Scotland: The Findings of a Survey of I.T. Provision in Scotland in the Early 1980s*. Edinburgh: Central Research Unit, Scottish Office.

Jones, R. (1980) The preventive and the penal: a comment on two models of intermediate treatment. *Journal of Adolescence 3*, 307–320.

Jones, R. (1981) Intermediate treatment, research and social policy. *Journal of Adolescence 4*, 339–352.

Jones, R. and Kerslake, A. (1979) *Intermediate Treatment and Social Work*. London: Heinemann.

Kilbrandon Committee (1964) *Report on Children and Young Persons, Scotland.* Cm 2306. Edinburgh: HMSO.

Knapp, M. and Fenyo, A. (1995) The cost and cost-effectiveness of IT. In A. Bottoms (1995).

Leissner, A., Powley, T. and Evans, D. (1977) *Intermediate Treatment: A Community-Based Action Research Study.* London: National Children's Bureau.

Lemert, E.M. (1972) *Human Deviance, Social Problems and Social Control.* Englewood Cliffs, New Jersey: Prentice-Hall.

Lilly, J.R. (1992) The English experience: intermediate treatment with juveniles. In J.M. Byrne, A.J. Lurigio and J. Petersilia (eds) *Smart Sentencing: The Emergence of Intermediate Sanctions.* Newbury Park, CA: Sage.

McClintock, F.M., Robertson A., Bennett-Emslie, G., van Teijlingen, E. and Wade, E. (1990) *Intermediate Treatment in Scotland: A Research Report.* Edinburgh: Social Work Services Group, Scottish Office.

Moos, R.H. (1973) Conceptualisation of human environments. *American Psychologist 28*, 20–29.

Moos, R.H. (1974) *Evaluating Treatment Environments: A Social Ecological Approach.* New York: Wiley.

NACRO (1989a) *Progress through Partnership. The Role of Statutory and Voluntary Agencies in the Funding and Management of Schemes for Juvenile Offenders Established under the DHSS Intermediate Treatment Initiative.* London: National Association for Care and Re-Settlement of Offenders, Juvenile Crime Section.

NACRO (1989b) *Replacing Custody: Findings from Two Census Surveys of Schemes for Juvenile Offenders Funded under the DHSS Intermediate Treatment Initiative, Covering the Period January to December, 1987.* London: National Association for Care and Re-Settlement of Offenders, Juvenile Crime Section.

NACRO (1991) *Seizing the Initiative: NACRO's Final Report on the DHSS Intermediate Treatment Initiative to Divert Juvenile Offenders from Care and Custody: 1983–1989.* London: National Association for Care and Re-Settlement of Offenders, Juvenile Crime Section.

Nellis, M. (1989) Juvenile justice and the voluntary sector. In R. Matthews (ed.) *Privatising Criminal Justice.* London: Sage.

Newsam, M. (1983) *Intermediate Treatment: A Model for Effective Practice.* Norwich: University of East Anglia in assocation with *Social Work Today.*

Robinson, C., Dixon, N. and Evans, S. (1988) *Falkirk District I.T. Project: Consumer Survey*. Edinburgh: Barnardo's Scotland.

Rutherford, A. (1986) *Growing out of Crime: Society and Young People in Trouble*. Harmondsworth: Penguin.

Skinner, A. (1985) *A Bibliography of Intermediate Treatment*. Leicester: National Association of Youth Clubs.

Stafford, E. (1984) *Does I.T. Work? A Study of the Effectiveness of Intermediate Treatment in Birmingham*. Birmingham: Birmingham Social Services Department.

Stone, M. (1984) *Intensive Intermediate Treatment for Persistent Young Offenders*. London: Northcote Trust in assocation with Department of Educational Studies, University of Surrey.

Thorpe, D., Smith, D., Green, C. and Paley, J. (1980) *Out of Care: The Community Support of Young Offenders*. London: Allen and Unwin.

Tutt, N. (1974) *Care or Custody: Community Homes and Treatment of Delinquency*. London: Dartman, Longman and Todd.

Walters, G. (1984) *Criminal Proceedings against Juveniles*. 1st ed. London: Oyez Longman.

Wasik, M. and Taylor, R.D. (1994) *Blackstone's Guide to the Criminal Justice Act 1991*. 2nd ed. London: Blackstone.

Wood, J. (1983) *Youth Clubs and Intermediate Treatment*. Leicester: National Association of Youth Clubs.

Chapter 8

Secure Units

Paul Littlewood

Introduction

The bland title for this chapter masks what is to many a particularly emotive issue; the practice of locking children up in institutions specifically designed (at least in part) for purposes of their containment. 'Secure units', 'secure accommodation', 'quiet rooms', 'separation rooms', 'withdrawal rooms' – these are all examples of what Cohen calls Controltalk; euphemisms coined by 'experts' in the interests of misrecognition (Cohen 1985, pp.273–281). When I proposed 'Children Behind Bars' as the title for an official report for publication, I was offered as preferred alternatives 'A Very Exceptional Measure', 'Restricting the Liberty of Children', or 'Care Appropriate to their Needs?'. I lamely plumped for the last. Only Milham *et al.*, in the first major study of secure accommodation in recent years, dared to break the barriers and refer explicitly to *Locking Up Children* (Milham, Bullock and Hosie 1978). As they wrote in their Foreword, 'turning keys is the distinguishing feature of security' (p.ix). One of the later studies (Harris and Timms 1993) takes the authors to task for this explicitness; but as we shall see, their criticism can in turn be questioned.

Relatively speaking, not many children are locked up in this way – according to Harris and Timms, 'only a few hundred' at any one time throughout Great Britain. No precise figures can be given, however, largely because of the covert nature of such institutions and their practices. Stewart and Tutt (1987), in trying to define custody, list time-out rooms, single separation rooms, police cells, short-term secure units, secure units linked to open units, closed psychiatric wards, detention centres, youth custody and young offenders' centres, and large long-term secure units – while pointing out that such practices as actual physical restraint, the denial of access to conventional clothing and the administration of drugs also effectively place children 'in custody'. We know, too, from exposures of 'pin-down', 'grounding' and similar practices in the early 1990s, that children can be effectively incarcerated even without any formal acknowledgement of the fact. Although pin-down as such may now be banned, it would seem likely that similar practices will continue to occur, if under other euphemisms, as hard-pressed and under-resourced staff seek immediate, pragmatic solutions to otherwise apparently intractable problems. So, the numbers of those actually in custody must remain unknown.

Much else is unknown about secure units, or was so until recently. Cawson, writing in the late 1980s, noted:

> It was particularly disturbing to find that there had been no major research on long term secure units since...the early 1970s. In spite of the millions which have been spent on the building programme, we are little wiser than we were in 1977 on the units' effects and their usefulness. (Cawson 1987, p.16)

One reason for this ignorance is the relatively high level of secrecy intrinsic to closed institutions; when people are locked away, they are also hidden from the public gaze. Another reason, more specifically associated with child custody, is the fear of publicity, or at least of sensationalist exposés through the mass media. Regimes, particularly in recent years, have frequently been the subject of exposures – even in the broadsheet press – of too much leniency on the one hand (the so-called 'crook's tour' episode: 'A teenage recidivist who missed two court appearances because he was taken on a £7000 African safari in an effort to make him change his ways was arrested again yesterday' (*The Guardian*, 29 December 1993); or allegedly cruel behaviour on the other ('Pinned down in purgatory: Kate, 15,...was put in 24-hour solitary confinement in a room with a bed, table and chair, without reading material, clad only in a mini-length nightdress' (*The Guardian*, 3 October 1990). Blumenthal introduces his study of the physical conditions of secure units by writing, 'Where institutions are as much open to criticism as the secure units for children in England and Wales are, it is not surprising to find highly developed defence mechanisms deployed by the persons involved... In this case the main technique employed is restriction of information' (Blumenthal 1985, p.1).

There are signs, however, that things are changing, both in terms of public debate and academic study. The inclusion in the Criminal Justice and Public Order Act (see Chapter 4 of this book) of plans to triple the number of secure unit places under English and Welsh local authorities to 235, on top of proposals to extend secure unit provision in the private sector, was widely publicised and debated in the context of claims about the rise in criminal offence rates among young people and the effect of the closure of many residential units. The debate focused on (1) the need to keep young offenders out of adult prisons, and (2) the level of effectiveness of a period in secure accommodation – two issues to be considered in more depth shortly. At a more scholarly level our awareness has also increased with the publication of three major studies – first Stewart and Tutt's exhaustive survey of children in custody in great Britain and Ireland (1987), followed by Kelly's detailed account of the tension between rhetoric and practice in one of Scotland's three secure units (1992), and Harris and Timms' elaborate exploration of the whole issue of secure accommodation, emanating from an earlier empirical study they had conducted (1993). The bulk of this chapter is a review of the principal findings and interpretations in these and other recent studies.

First, however, there is another problem of definition to consider, which is crucial to the whole issue of child custody itself, and from which the issue derives much of its emotive power; that is, what constitutes a 'child' in the first place. Since the publication of Ariès' ground-breaking text (1962), the sociological conception of childhood as a social construction, rather than a 'natural' stage in the lifecycle, has virtually become an orthodoxy. As James and Prout demonstrate, while 'The twentieth century is said to be "century of the child" and perhaps at no other time have children been so highly profiled' (James and Prout 1990, p.1), this has led to a new dimension in the 'mismatch between the "real" and the "ideal"...the extent to which the 'ideal is having to be currently reassessed within the public domain' (1990, p.2).

Ariès' own analysis has been much criticised but the basic point has become central to the analysis of changing conceptions of childhood, particularly since the industrial revolution: by elongating the status of children by juridically depriving them of adult status and instead providing them with an ever more complex battery of legal, educational, medical, psychological, psychiatric and penal treatments and control mechanisms, we have continually reconstructed images of children and their needs, interests and potentialities, while denying them authority in determining much of their own destinies. Central to these reconstructions are ever more elaborate conceptions of 'problem' children as we seek to identify and classify how children should behave, how they should 'develop' and what attitudes they should express. Thus we have also created and exacerbated a series of dilemmas, not just for them but ourselves as well, as to how to reconcile our 'expert' (and often conflicting) views of children's 'needs' and 'best interests' with the fact that children are also social actors, capable of assigning meanings, making choices and decisions and acting in what they regard as their best interests. In other words, we are forever caught in the trap of defending and seeking in some cases to extend children's rights while at the same time devising ever more schemes to reduce the scope of such rights, from restrictions of child labour to raising the school leaving age, from determining their own sexualities to increasing pressure to place ever larger numbers of children in custodial institutions.

Conflicting legal definitions of 'what is a child' abound. Stewart and Tutt point to the array of definitions of both when a child can be can be assumed to understand right from wrong, and when an individual can be treated as a fully responsible adult and not afforded special treatment, within the British Isles alone (Stewart and Tutt 1987, pp.6–7). In the Irish Republic one can be charged with a criminal offence from 7 years; in Scotland, from 8; in Northern Ireland – and until very recently, in England and Wales, from 10. Now, however, there has been the Law Lords' shifting of the age of criminal responsibility from 10 back to 14 – although with the proviso that the law needs changing (*The Independent*, 17 March 1995). The age of adult responsibility is currently 16 in Scotland and 17 in England, Wales and the whole of Ireland. In much of continental Europe, both the minimum age for prosecution for a criminal offence and the age at which individuals are held fully responsible as adults tend to be higher.

More generally, particularly in the press, there is the frequent equation of the terms 'children' (in the legal sense used above) and 'young people', which further illustrates the slippery nature of the concepts and issues involved. This confusion is driven by the very ambivalence in the shifting construction of childhood. On the one hand there is the belief that, at least in some circumstances, chronologically young children are to some degree aware that what they have done is wrong or anti-social, and must be both punished and seen to be punished; and on a more pragmatic note, 'society' too must be protected from them, at least until they have earned the error of their ways. On the other hand there is the 'child-saving' interest in protecting the young from the potentially pernicious influence of adults – either at home or in custodial institutions designed for older people – or from what on occasion children might be thought to intend to do. Frequently coupled with this interest are the beliefs that socially immature people need to be protected from themselves, and might best be 'treated' in a custodial setting. This ambivalence lies behind the subtitle of Harris and Timms' book on secure accommodation: *Between Hospital and Prison or Thereabouts?*.

The rest of this chapter will concentrate on what happens to those under 16 or 17 in the context of custody in Britain. I will restrict my review to the criteria used for the placement of children in secure units, the sorts of children sent to them, units' policies and practices of treatment and preparation and activities of their staff.

Criteria for placement in secure units

During the first two decades of their existence, there were no explicit and consistent sets of criteria for determining who qualified for admission to secure units in Britain. In 1982 the Children's Legal Centre published a highly critical report, pointing to the rapid increase in the numbers of children sent to them (including many with little or no history of offending), the absence of clear criteria and the fact that then current practice contravened Article 5.4 of the European Convention on Human Rights by permitting the holding of children without a formally constituted legal hearing (Children's Legal Centre 1982). A series of studies all indicated that placement was often arbitrary and unsuitable for many of the children concerned (Milham *et al.* 1978; Cawson and Martell 1979; Petrie 1980). As a direct result of the CLC report, explicit criteria were finally introduced in the early 1980s, and have since been subject to some elaboration and modification. But, as Stewart and Tutt's study most clearly indicates, the rules and guidelines informing decisions as to who may be held in a secure unit and by what authority are highly complex, subject to change and often very vague. They are therefore open to considerable variations in interpretation.

It is not within the scope of this chapter to give precise details but in general terms the criteria presently in operation are as follows. In

England and Wales authorisation can be granted if a child in the care of a local authority either has a history of absconding, is likely to abscond again and in so doing is likely to suffer significant harm; or if such child, if not kept in secure accommodation, is likely to harm him or herself or others. A child may be held for up to three months at the first hearing and up to six months on renewal, and should be released when the reasons behind the authorisation no longer exist. Authorisation can also be granted for children remanded while awaiting trial or sentence, and for those serving sentences under Section 53 of the Children and Young Persons Act 1933. In Scotland authorisation may be granted when either the Children's Hearings or Sheriff have established that a child is in need of compulsory care; and then, that he or she either has a history of absconding and is likely to abscond again, and in which case his or her physical, mental or moral welfare will be at risk; or is likely to injure him or herself or others if not held in secure accommodation. The only time limit imposed in Scotland is a requirement to review – initially after three months and thereafter nine months (Stewart and Tutt 1987, p.177). Authorisation may also be granted for children found guilty of having committed offences under Sections 206 and 413 of the Criminal Procedure (Scotland) Act 1975, children awaiting trial for serious offences, and children remanded under unruly certificates.

The criteria applying on both sides of the Border are now largely compatible, although the Children's Hearings System in Scotland, through which many children referred to secure units pass under Section 44(1) of the Social Work (Scotland) Act 1968, reflects the much more central role accorded to the welfare model for dealing with children (and hence perhaps the more open time limits for custody), rather than the justice model which is relatively more characteristic in England and Wales. The criteria are, however, loosely phrased and open to a considerable breadth in interpretation; in particular, determining the likelihood of a child absconding, or of harming him or herself or others, or assessing the degree of mental moral or physical risk, all involve a high degree of subjective judgement, to be made on often scanty information. Although the processes of decision making are now undoubtedly more tightly controlled and subject to scrutiny and review, the opaqueness of the new criteria still leaves considerable room for the sorts of idiosyncratic and arbitrary judgement which characterised many of the decisions to place children in secure units before the criteria were introduced.

Children placed in secure units

Another crucial aspect involved in the development of admissions criteria is the emphasis that such a development places on the type of child. This too is linked to the increased application of the welfare model, in that the identification of types of children suitable for and in need of secure accommodation diminishes the relative importance of (1) their having committed a certain sort of act resulting in a judicial judgement, and (2) the alternative or additional understanding that the 'problem' might lie outside the child and in a set of circumstances resulting in the child's problematic behaviour. To illustrate this point, persistent absconding is a common feature in the careers of those placed in secure units; but as Milham *et al.* point out, '[I]t is the nature of a child's residential experience that makes him an absconder...boys run because of the places they are in' (1978, p.17). This sort of finding, however, tends to be neglected as the philosophy underlying the committal of children to secure units becomes yet more geared to notions of treatment of types of children with types of problem. Thorpe *et al.* note that 'the therapeutic function laid on residential institutions by the new legislation [of the 1960s] had a net widening effect as these establishments could claim to exist to help children in need rather than train and control young offenders' (1980, cited in Stewart and Tutt 1987, p.71). We shall see shortly, however, that therapy and treatment in secure units tend in practice to fall far short of stated goals.

All of the major studies of secure units consider the issue of which children are sent to secure units and raise serious questions about the appropriateness of such placements for many of the children involved. No doubt, some of the children have to be locked up because of the nature of the offences they have committed, and others have behaved in ways which previous care agencies have been unable to control. But a significant number appear to have been placed in secure units not so much because of their personal behaviour – they appear to be little different from children who have not been so placed – but rather because of the ways they have been dealt with in previous institutions and the ways in which the proposal for secure placement have been conducted. Milham *et al.* stress both these aspects in saying that children in secure units 'are rarely propelled by inner drives and that much of their conduct is largely engendered by, and understandable in the context of institutions in which they shelter. It is also clear that the majority of children in the secure units are not intractable cases that differ markedly from other children in open conditions'. They also cite Cawson's earlier finding that 'the factor correlating most strongly with entry was not anything to do with the child's need but was the number of letters written to request a place' (Milham *et al.* 1978, p.52). The clear implication here is that principal causes behind many placements lie not in the children but other caring agencies and the processes of referral themselves. Similarly Cawson and Martell found 'that a small number of establishments influenced a large number of referrals; that referrals could not be fully explained in terms of behaviour; and that previous short term, disrupted placement patterns suggested a low tolerance of these children in other forms of residential care' (Cawson and Martell 1979, p.144). In a later study of referrals to one secure unit, it was concluded that 'nothing clearly indicated why certain candidates (for secure accommodation) were suitable and others were not. From this one can infer that the number of children locked up...is more a function of the number of beds available than of some need found in a number of our adolescent population' (Littlewood 1987, p.14). Reforms in the provision of residential care for children and in referrals policy would not appear to have altered the situation. Referring to the 'logical and empirical impossibility of providing an unambiguous operational definition of the child who should...enter secure accommodation', Harris and Timms conclude from 'talking to the experts', 'either that the mere existence of secure accommodation provokes its usage or that the pressures which led to a unit's construction in the first place continue to influence that usage' (1993, pp.99–100).

Treatment policies and practices

Wilkie and Westwood suggest that there are several purposes underlying secure accommodation in the child-care system: containment, control, care, treatment and rehabilitation. As Stewart and Tutt point out, however, '[I]n their implementation these objectives are difficult to combine, creating difficulties for practice' – especially in the case of long-stay provision' (Wilkie and Westwood 1985, cited in Stewart and Tutt 1987, p.65).

Clearly the primary purpose of secure units is containment: 'In a secure unit, the first essential of the arrangements is continuous and effective control' (Department of Health and Social Security 1977). Surveys of the range of security features and measures in secure units all note their overall prison-like nature: 'Walking round a secure unit, it feels like a sensorily deprived environment, controlled by the routinised locking and unlocking of doors' (Stewart and Tutt 1987, pp.148–149; see also Milham *et al.* 1978; Blumenthal 1985). Kelly gives a more detailed description of the security arrangements in one unit: 'In essence it remained a prison which is clear from the high level of physical security it imposed on inmates.' She writes of the doors and internal iron-barred gates which could only be unlocked by authorised staff members, the cell-like bedrooms with steel doors locked from the outside and surveillance peepholes, the isolation unit, the two small outdoor yards surrounded by walls approximately fifteen feet high, the electronic alarm system, the cramped conditions and the sparse and poor-quality furnishings (Kelly 1992, pp.51–56); 'the building itself incorporated a philosophy of control and surveillance...the unit exerted a very high level of control over the children's movements, activities, possessions, privacy and time...visits...were always supervised by members of staff...all in going and outgoing mail was read by staff and all phone calls monitored' (1992, pp. 140, 142, 143).

The development and implementation of treatment policies can only be analysed and understood in this carceral context. In the summary report of the research on which Kelly's account is based I wrote, 'any treatment-oriented practices were severely impeded by a pervasive atmosphere of containment' (Littlewood 1987, p.17). Kelly explores this in greater depth in her later book on the relationship between rhetoric and practice, in which she describes the muddled attempts to develop a treatment policy and the failure to implement it by staff inadequately trained and prepared, and divided among themselves as to the role of treatment in such an overtly custodial setting:

> Although staff found it impossible to identify and articulate a shared treatment goal as part of the ethos of the unit, it was nevertheless accurate to describe the unit as having been conceived of rhetorically as a treatment centre; moreover, most staff clearly resented the dominant custodial ideas they saw behind the current regime and would have preferred to provide more indi-

> vidual 'treatment' even at the cost of 'security' – despite their inability to provide it. (Kelly 1992, p.128)

What happened in effect was the controlled management of children.

> It seems that despite official construction of the unit as a treatment centre, and the staff's idealistic commitment to treatment notions, the daily organisation of the unit had few of the many aspects thought to be typical of treatment institutions and displayed largely custodial features... Locking up children was construed as being for their own good and to teach them self-control... Far from attempting to solve individuals' personal problems, staff seemed mainly concerned to see that the institution ran smoothly. (1992, p.153)

Few of the other studies of secure units give much detail about treatment policies and practices, although Stewart and Tutt's survey suggests that 'most units did seem to operate regimes which were based on explicit principles', such as behaviour modification and individualised programmes. 'A number of regimes were frankly eclectic...[using] a variety of behaviour modification, counselling and group treatment methods', according to one institution (Stewart and Tutt 1987, pp.153–157). But responses to questionnaires hardly indicate the nature of actual practice and may be closer to Kelly's 'rhetoric'.

Staffing

Those studies of secure units which consider issues other than just the children placed in them note, as far as care workers are concerned, the relatively low status accorded to the work of the staff within them, their low levels of remuneration, their lack of child-care training and the high levels of stress involved in the work itself. According to Milham *et al.*, there was

> a dearth in applications from staff in other children's establishments... It is argued, not without reason, that staff who are familiar with difficult and demanding children in open conditions might rapidly come to doubt the need for security. It seems that staff with no previous child-care experience adapt more easily to the demands of the task, particularly because they accept more readily ideas that the children are difficult and dangerous and that security is essential...many of the staff who join units have little

> or no experience of the sorts of behaviour problems that the children present. (1978, pp.128, 131)

A similar point is made by Harris and Timms, who found that many staff 'are untrained sub-professional employees, marginal to the main enterprise of their agency yet with the awesome duty of holding against their will some of the most difficult and disturbed of the agency's clientele' (Harris and Timms 1993, p.85).

Stewart and Tutt go some way towards explaining the lack of training by suggesting that

> recruitment criteria and training are affected by the dilemma in which many employers find themselves; it seems against all good child-care principles to lock up children and yet it is necessary to provide and staff secure units. This dilemma prevents many committed child-care workers from applying for such work and may therefore lead to recruitment of inexperienced and untrained applicants. (Stewart and Tutt 1987, p.79)

Kelly suggests that it is the relative lack of training which contributes to a sense of low status. She found that

> [c] are staff were considerably less qualified than teaching staff... It is this relative under-qualification which contributes to a tendency for residential care staff to feel they have a limited standing compared with teachers and senior staff – a feeling shared in the unit by the instructors. Of the 13 care staff interviewed, only 3 had a social work qualification. And, like care staff elsewhere, they were faced with obstacles to their becoming qualified. The secure unit did not provide access to encourage professional training for more than a few; and there was no in-service training. (Kelly 1992, p.61)

No doubt this relative lack of professional expertise contributed to the gap she notes between the rhetoric of treatment and actual everyday practice; '[a]ll staff felt that the influence of the [psychologist and psychiatric] consultants was non-existent or "negligible" in deciding how to handle children and in the running of the unit' (1992, p.114). Harris and Timms also note the distance between the 'sharp-end' workers and the members of senior management they interviewed: 'none could produce a training strategy to help staff manage discretion, enhance their skills in, for example, behaviour management or conflict regulation, or integrate their units with those broader departmental child-care policies from which they seemed to be far removed' (Harris and Timms 1993, p.85).

None of this account of the lack of training of care staff is intended, however, to imply that most if not all such staff do actually and actively 'care' for the children in their charge. The fact that some of the children interviewed in various reports appear to have built close, enduring relationships with individual members of staff, often after long stretches in their lives with no such dependable relationships, is testimony to the fact that life in secure units is not always as bad as one might fear when reading some of the more detailed accounts about them. This is a point close to the perspective taken by Harris and Timms, consideration of which provides the basis for my conclusion.

Concluding comments

Most of the sociologically informed accounts of secure units adopt a clear stance: the practice of locking up children is to be strongly discouraged, given the arbitrary nature of selection procedures, the prison-like nature of containment, the lack of development of well-grounded and effective treatment policies and the strong inference that many of the children are locked up in this way because the places, like mountains, are there. Unlike mountains, however, they can be disposed of; and as Harris and Timms's study demonstrates, while some local authorities provide secure units, other do not and presumably do not feel the need to do so. This may be in part because the latter can avail themselves of the secure unit facilities of the former – which in advertising them justify their existence. But, given the fact that there are far more children not in secure units who present similar behavioural problems to those inside them, together with the marked differences in policies and practices between 'experts' concerning secure units evident among different care agencies, it is clear that the provision of so many places, geographically so unevenly distributed, is in large part the consequence of political pressure and court disposal policy, which push the care system into establishing and maintaining secure units.

Harris and Timms consider such arguments in terms of the purposes of secure accommodation.

> Is its purpose to provide an insecure youngster with psychological 'security', to provide the rest of us – adults and children alike – with 'security' from the youngster, or both? To some, it is the former; to others of a more cynical bent the latter, albeit sometimes disguised as the former, and with the secondary purpose of meeting the self-aggrandising demands of child-care professionals as they engage in the endless pursuit of ever more children in need of their expertise and, in consequence, ever more resources. (Harris and Timms 1993, p.ix)

By taking the latter stance, they argue, the authors of the major studies have misconstrued the purpose of secure units:

> In secure accommodation the penal and the therapeutic, the controlling and the caring converge, and the resulting ambiguity is central to the system's logic. Secure accommodation is the point at which the protection of children and the protection of others against those same children merge into a single carceral proposal. (1993, p.4)

Secure units are a combined outcome of the historical trends which separate juvenile from adult offender and which seek to identify the needs of certain children.

> Secure accommodation, in embracing not only different categories of offender but also non-offenders, seeks simultaneously to meet the needs of disturbed or unfortunate youngsters and to inject discipline and structure into the lives of the deviant young. For secure accommodation is precisely the locus in which the question of whether a child has committed an offence or is in some other way problematic ceases to matter. (1993, p.6)

But 'ceases to matter' to whom? Things and issues don't 'matter' in the abstract or in general; they 'matter' to particular groups of people with particular interests. The authors' failure to identify these interests is an important lapse in their otherwise profound interpretation. This comment does not just apply to a particular passage in the book but to their general approach; later, in returning to their criticism of Milham and his colleagues in particular they write: 'to them secure accommodation is primarily punishment disguised as care; to us...it "is" both simultaneously, neither hospital nor prison but between the two – or thereabouts' (p.50). Again one is left wondering whether that is what secure accommodation means, not just to scholarly researchers but to those confined within it, both children and staff. From the studies surveyed here, it would seem that for many of these people, Milham *et al.*'s understanding is the more accurate. If that is the case, the act of placing children who have not committed serious offences in secure units cannot be defended, even if one of their functions is 'care'.

References

Ariès, P. (1962) *Centuries of Childhood*. London: Jonathan Cape.

Blumenthal, G. (1985) *Development of Secure Units in Child Care*. Aldershot: Gower Press.

Cawson, P. (1987) Children behind locked doors. *Childright 37*, 16–18.

Cawson, P. and Martell, M. (1979) *Children Referred to Closed Units*. Department of Health and Social Security Statistics and Research Division, Research Report No. 5. London: HMSO.

Children's Legal Centre (1982) *Locked Up in Care: A Report on the Use of Secure Accommodation for Young People in Care*. London: Children's Legal Centre.

Cohen, S. (1985) *Visions of Social Control*. Cambridge: Polity Press.

Department of Health and Social Security (1977) *Community Homes Design Guidance – A Small Secure Unit*. London: HMSO.

Harris, R. and Timms, N. (1993) *Secure Accommodation in Child Care: Between Hospital and Prison or Thereabouts?* London: Routledge.

James, A. and Prout, A. (1990) Introduction. In A. James and A. Prout (eds) *Constructing and Reconstructing Childhood*. Basingstoke: Falmer Press.

Kelly, B. (1992) *Children Inside: Rhetoric and Practice in a Locked Institution for Children*. London: Routledge.

Littlewood, P. (1987) *Care Appropriate to Their Needs? Summary of a Sociological Study of a Secure Unit for Children in Scotland (1982–6)*. Scottish Office Central Research Unit Papers, Social Work Services Group, Scottish Education Department. Edinburgh: Scottish Office.

Milham, S., Bullock, R. and Hosie, K. (1978) *Locking Up Children: Secure Provision within the Child-Care System*. Farnborough: Saxon House.

Petrie, K. (1980) *The Nowhere Boys: A Comparative Study of Open and Closed Residential Treatment*. Aldershot: Gower.

Stewart, G. and Tutt, N. (1987) *Children in Custody*. Aldershot: Avebury.

Thorpe, D., Smith, D., Green, D. and Paley, J. (1980) *Out of Care*. London: Allen and Unwin.

Wilkie, J. and Westwood, S. (1985) Co-education and the treatment of disturbed adolescents with special reference to Glenthorne Y.T.C. Birmingham: Glenthorne Publications, No. 4.

Chapter 9

Restorative Juvenile Justice

A Way to Restore Justice in Western European Systems?

Lode Walgrave

Juvenile justice in western Europe: Different ways to cope with the same problems

Generally speaking, all European countries do have special regimes to react against juveniles who committed offences. All special regimes are inspired by a welfare approach: punishments are to be avoided as much as possible and to be adapted to the special needs of young people.

Two factors play a role in arguing for such regimes. First, the age of minority is used as a diminishment of guilt, as minors are considered less 'capable of understanding and willing' (terms used in Italy). This excuse of minority (term used in France) leads to the reduction of punishments compared to those applicable to adults. Secondly, it is believed that young offenders can, more than adults, be influenced positively. Punishments or measures should therefore be pedagogic. In juvenile justice, the retributive character has faded away and the instrumentalist rehabilitative approach has become predominant.

Despite the common basic assumptions, there are major differences in the way countries elaborate their own system (Mehlbye and Walgrave 1995). Time and again the struggle with the very difficult combination of a welfare approach in a judicial structure surfaces. Everywhere it shows that the systems have undergone a great deal of doctoring. The Eastern European countries are in a period of deep transition, so that information about them would risk to be irrelevant. But in other countries also, the permanent search for a better balance between the justice and the welfare thinking provokes steady modifications. That is why our detailed comment will be based on a limited number of countries, about which we have recent and reliable information (Mehlbye and Walgrave 1995).

The comparisons of juvenile justice will be made following four topics.

1. the age categories to which the special regime of judicial intervention applies,
2. the agencies imposing coercive measures to minor delinquents,
3. possible special procedures for the prosecution of minor delinquents, with special attention for educational concerns,
4. specific (educative or punitive) measures taken against minors who committed an offence.

Civil and penal majority coincide, but the transitional age categories are very different

Five different means of dealing with young people who commit offences can be identified in the European Union (see Mehlbye and Walgrave 1995 for a fuller discussion of the different age categories employed throughout Europe and the implications these have for the administration of justice with regard to young offenders):

1. a pure welfare approach,
2. a Welfare approach with some exceptions for penal interventions,
3. a specific system of juvenile penal law,
4. a penal intervention with exceptions for educative concerns, and
5. a purely retributive system.

In all countries, the age of penal majority corresponds with the civil majority. Slight exceptions to this logical classification exist in some countries like England and Wales (also in Spain or Portugal), and they betray an element of social-pedagogic attitude with regard to young adults. The most far reaching exception concerns Germany, where the 'Heranwachsenden' (young adults of 18 up to 20 years of age) are put under the jurisdiction of the juvenile court and may be prosecuted according to the Jugendgerichtsgesetz (the Juvenile Court Law).

The age of criminal responsibility varies a lot. In England young delinquents from the age of 10 onwards can be proceeded against for their offence. In Scotland this is theoretically possible from the age of

8, though this is done only exceptionally in practice. In Belgium (as in Luxembourg) a youngster can only be prosecuted from the age of 16 onwards. In practice, however, minors are seldom subjected to penal law, but many so-called protective measures are often imposed with a punitive overtone.

Before this minimum age, interventions are purely welfare-oriented. Also children who committed an offence are treated or (re)educated and not punished. In such cases forced treatment can alternatively be the case. Mostly the families are involved in the intervention.

Between the minimum age of criminal responsibility and the age of penal majority, the age categories and the kind of possible interventions are rather different. In most countries (Belgium, France, the Netherlands, Scotland, England and Wales) the age of 16 is crucial. Before it, the welfare approach is mostly the rule, and the penal approach the exception. After 16 the punitive approach becomes more important.

But even then major nuances and differences remain. In Denmark, for instance, the regular criminal judge is competent for delinquents from 15 onwards, but pedagogic and social oriented exceptions and procedures are provided for. On the contrary, the Belgian juvenile court initially remains competent up to the age of 18, unless in the abovementioned exception, and can, theoretically, only impose protective measures, as for the younger children or for regular welfare cases).

This great variety in age categories and judicial regimes is a first indication of the confusion in finding a system to respond adequately to the transitional period between the child, presumed to be innocent and not punishable and the adult, presumed to be responsible and punishable.

Special agencies (mostly juvenile courts) impose coercive measures on delinquent minors

With the exception of Denmark (and the other Scandinavian countries) and Scotland, a specialised court for minors exists everywhere, but their organisation and authorities differ.

In Belgium, France, Italy, and the Netherlands (and in most other countries of the European Union) the juvenile courts are also authorised with regard to so-called civil or protective matters, i.e. imposing measures for the protection of the education circumstances of the minors. This also betrays the explicit welfare or educative orientation of these courts and of the juvenile penal law that directs their interventions. In Italy, France and the Netherlands it is stated explicitly that juvenile penal law, in the first place, has educative objectives, and that all punishments should be imposed, as much as possible aiming at (re)education. In Belgium penal law for juveniles does not exist and the juvenile delinquents are approached by the judicial juvenile protection.

In Germany, the jurisdiction over juvenile delinquents is strictly separated from welfare interventions, though some measures of the juvenile court do overlap with those taken by the welfare agencies.

In most countries a professional judge has his seat in the Juvenile Court (or the 'Children's Court' according to the terminology in France and the Netherlands), but sometimes, like in Italy, he is assisted by two non-professional observers. In France and in Germany the juvenile penal jurisdiction provides three steps: the professional judge sits alone when the cases are less serious; the more serious cases are judged by an intermediate court composed of the judge and 'assesseurs'. For the most serious category of offences the minor is referred to the 'Cour d'Assises des mineurs' or to the 'Jugendkammer'.

In England and Wales there has been no confusion between the 'care-jurisdiction' and the criminal jurisdiction since 1989. The 'Family proceedings panel of the magistrates' Court' is authorised for the first, and the Youth Court for the latter. The Youth Court consists of three lay magistrates, advised by a legally qualified clerk, and only judges youngsters who committed an offence. The pedagogic motivation remains very important for the sentence, but more attention seems to go to individualisation, persistence, and seriousness of the delinquency and on representing the community in a sensible, common-sense way. In practice, the justice-orientation seems to be stronger than the welfare-orientation.

In Scotland and Denmark no special court exists for minors.

In Denmark the Local Welfare Authorities, that are also dealing with all kinds of social aid (the disabled, elderly people, etc.), are fully authorised until the age of 15. They primarily offer help. If coercive measures are taken, the parents and the children have the aid of a lawyer. From the age of 15 onwards all delinquents appear, in principle, before the regular judge, but up to the age of 18 special procedure rules are followed, so that the welfare authorities can exercise a strong influence on the jurisdiction. Also special rules and regimes for the implementation of punishments apply for youngsters.

In Scotland the Children's Hearing is the most important institution in the approach of juvenile delinquents up to the age of 18. With the exception of offenders of very serious and technical offences (who are heard in the regular courts), all minor offenders are signalled to the Reporter who could decide to refer the case to the Children's Hearing System. Cases of neglect and other malpractice in education can also be signalled there. A hearing consists of three non-professionals who are given a kind of training when they are appointed and are regularly counselled. This institution can only decide whether the child is in need of compulsory measures of care and about the contents of these measures. Co-operation with the social work departments, that are also charged with general welfare work, is very intense. From the age of 16, juvenile delinquents may appear in the criminal courts, unless they had been under the supervision of the children's hearing before. In that case they can remain under this authority up to their eighteenth birthday.

Welfare orientation provokes special procedural rules in prosecuting minor offenders

All countries provide special procedure rules for the prosecution of juvenile delinquents. Often these youth-oriented rules apply from the beginning of the procedure, on the police-level.

In almost all countries the police have but few discretionary powers, so that they cannot take special measures against minors. Only in the Netherlands and England is this different.

In the Netherlands the police can autonomously decide to classify a case. After an informal warning, the minor can be referred to a diversion programme or a formal report can be made that is sent to the Public Prosecutor. In recent years the diversion-possibility has been used a lot.

In England and Wales the police can classify the case. After an informal warning they can pronounce a formal cautioning, or they can refer the case to the Crown Prosecution Service aiming at further prosecution. Here too cautioning is used a lot, especially up to the age of 16. Often informal conditions are added, such as reparation or supervision. Many decisions are taken in consultation with the social sector. Therefore, in many districts 'inter-agency juvenile bureaux' were established where regularly consultation takes place between the police, social services, education and youth services.

Although elsewhere the police play a less outspoken role, special arrangements are to be mentioned: in Denmark and Scotland, for instance, the welfare agencies can be involved from the very beginning of the police investigation. In Belgium, special youth brigades exist in most of the police forces that are often staffed by police-officers with a diploma in social work (or related diploma); many informal consultations about specific files take place between the police and the diverse welfare and/or educative institutions. The Public Prosecutor is not always well informed about this.

In all countries the Public Prosecutor is the decisive instigator of the prosecution of youngsters. He can dismiss the case, refer the case to welfare agencies, with or without suspension of prosecution and he can decide to prosecute.

In the Netherlands and in Germany, the Public Prosecutor can also apply the 'dismiss under conditions' (a form of probation). In the Netherlands, a fine or a limited alternative sanction is imposed. This decision of the Public Prosecutor can only be taken after consultation with, or with the approval of the Children's Judge. Therefore, in most court districts tripartite meetings are organised where next to the Public Prosecutor and the Children's Judge, representatives of the Child Protection Council are also present. In Germany, the option for a diversionary procedure has granted the public prosecutor with a lot of diverse power, like proposing educational conditions, social skills training, community service, mediation, fines, etc. The juvenile can always refuse these propositions, in which case, a normal prosecution can follow. Moreover, juvenile prosecutor can propose to the judge more simplified hearings than the formal charges.

In Italy, after the preliminary investigation phase, a preliminary hearing is organised where a definitive decision is taken whether to prosecute the case or not. There can also be decided to impose alternatives to detention, such as fines, semi-detention, or probation.

Concerning the preliminary investigation phase it is important to mention that the Belgian and French juvenile or children's judges conduct the investigation phase themselves (with a few exceptions). This is accounted for with the argument that the welfare approach of youngsters is a specialisation that requires continuity in approach. Consequently, the provisional measures, allegedly taken for the investigation, quite often serve as actual measures but without a formal sentence. In Scotland, however, a very strict division is kept between the observation of the facts and the pronouncement of the measure, but also with the argument of a very strong welfare approach of the Children's Hearing System.

In the preliminary phase not only inquiries are made about the facts as such, but also about the social and psychological circumstances of the juvenile offenders, and this in all countries. This information is supplied, either by an own service specialised in working with juvenile courts (as in Belgium and France) or by a general extra-judicial service.

Preventive custody indicates that the safety risks are explicitly assessed more serious than the need for educative measures. In almost all countries preventive custody can be applied but always under stricter conditions than when applied to adults. It is always stipulated that this measure should be executed in separate institutions or sections of institutions, separated from the adults. A very strict time-limit is almost always employed. In Denmark consultation with the welfare authorities should proceed. It is remarkable that Italy also provides the possibility of house arrest. In Belgium, theoretically speaking, custody does not exist. Yet, a preliminary measure exists that states that detention in a house of custody is possible when no suitable place is available in a regular institution for minors, and then only for a maximum of 15 days.

It is quite clear that these special procedural rules are inspired by concerns on the greater vulnerability of young people and by the option for rehabilitative judicial intervention towards them.

Rehabilitative options lead to special measures and punishments for juvenile offenders

The following table gives a brief overview of the measures and punishments that a court can impose on juvenile offenders. This table reveals a few striking characteristics.

In England and Wales it is not possible that a minor delinquent ends up in the welfare-circuit by force. The one that is caught for an offence will be dealt with explicitly on that basis. Yet, it is possible that among the conditions or requirements that are often linked to certain sentences, welfare-oriented conditions are also implied, such as being treated or helped.

Belgium and Scotland do not dispose of a specialised juvenile penal law. In the first place this is due to the fact that the approach to juvenile delinquency is almost exclusively in welfare terms. Consequently, cases

Table 9.1 Coercive measures or punishments, imposed on offending minors

B: till age 17	*DK: till age 17*	*SC: till age 15*	*NL: age 12–17*	*F: age 13–17*	*I: age 14–17*	*ENG: age 10–17*	*D: age 14–17*
Refer to welfare Reprimand Supervision (+conditions) Placement in family/ institution Placement in closed institution (max. till age 20)	Till age 14: All kinds of ambulant and residential care	Till age 15: Discharge Supervision order → social work Residential supervision → social work	Refer to welfare Jurisdiction as child in danger	Back to family Reprimand Supervision order (+ conditions) Placement in family/ institutions	Pardon Dismissal for inability to understand and → welfare		Educational measures: Educational directives Educational guidance Institutional education

Table 9.1 Coercive measures or punishments, imposed on offending minors (continued)

B: till age 17	*DK: till age 17*	*SC: till age 15*	*SC: till age 15*	*F: age 13–17*	*I: age 14–17*	*ENG: age 10–17*	*D: age 14–17*
	Age 15–17: Penal court with special rules for juveniles Suspended charge → welfare Suspended sentence (+conditions a.o. → welfare) Fine In institution Imprisonment in 'socio-pedagogic' institution (max. 8 years) Imprisonment		Reprimand Fine Probation Custody in 'correctional school' (max. 6 months)	Service order Fine Probation Custody (max. ½ of adults)	Probation (max. 1 year or 3 years) custody in 'approved schools' (max. ⅔ of adults)	Discharge (+ conditions) Measures on parents (bind over; fine; compensation order) Attendance centre (max. 24/36 hrs) Supervision (+ requirements) From age 15: Detention in Young Offenders Institution From age 16: Probation (+ requirements) From age 16: Community Service Detention (from age 10/14/16)	Disciplinary measures: Reprimand Disciplinary orders Custody (max. 4 weeks) Imprisonment: Suspended Imprisonment (max. 2 years) + probation orders Imprisonment (min. 6 months; max. 5 years)
Age 16–17: Referral to adults court		From age 8: Adults court for very serious and technical offences	Age 16–17: Referral to adults court				

are referred to to a regular criminal judge if the welfare-approach is inadequate. In practice, this is rather exceptional.

Denmark occupies a somewhat special place in this table. In principle, youngsters from 15 onwards are sentenced by the regular criminal court. But since there are so many special procedure rules and measures provided for minors, it seems more appropriate to classify Denmark among the countries with a special juvenile penal law.

Notwithstanding the major differences in the formal systems, the similarities are striking as well.

In almost every country a double trace can be followed with regard to juvenile delinquents, that is, one can almost everywhere choose for a more punitive or a more welfare-oriented approach. This is especially obvious in Denmark (from 15 onwards), the Netherlands, France, Italy and Germany where the (juvenile) judge can decide to react on either the offence as such, or to consider it as a sign of a welfare problem and to work on that or to have worked on that. In Scotland the double trace is very explicit, but up to 16 the welfare-orientation is very strong whereas afterwards the penal law becomes significantly more important.

Theoretically, Belgium only uses the welfare-oriented approach, but in practice some welfare measures turn out to be factual punitive measures. Only in England and Wales the accent is more exclusively put on retribution, yet many welfare considerations can be used in the jurisdiction and in the imposed conditions.

In every country the same gradation in possible measures exists:

- Cautioning.
- Supervision with conditions. The possible conditions mentioned are more or less the same, viz. accept supervision and/or guiding, do one or other form of reparation, a form of unpaid service to the community. The extent to which supervision and conditions are limited in time can differ. The technical quality of supervision and guiding also depends on the local means, and development in social work and traditions.
- Placement in families or in institutions. Juvenile delinquents can be taken away from their home environment and consigned to the care of an acknowledged, more adequate educative environment. Also here local differences can be discerned in the duration of the placement and in the technical contents of the implementation.

- Placement in a closed institution. Everywhere, juvenile delinquents can be separated from the community, but this still happens in the name of an educative motive. Therefore, one speaks of special institutions for youngsters also there where a real punitive measure is meant. In Belgium an educative measure can be imposed in a 'closed section of a public institution'; in Denmark a 'socio-pedagogic institution' replaces prison; in the Netherlands the closed juvenile punitive sanction is implemented in a 'correctional school'; in Italy this happens in 'approved schools', in England and Wales youngsters from the age of 15 onwards can be confined in a Young Offenders Institution and in Germany short disciplinary custody or imprisonment happen in special Youth Custody Houses or in Youth Prisons. Everywhere the measure is meant to be a compromise between a kind of safety measure on behalf of the community, a punishment with regard to the delinquent and an educative objective. Because of the serious deprivation of liberty, the time-limit of this measure is well indicated.
- Eventually youngsters from the age of 16 onwards can be detained in a normal prison, but also here a special regime is used.

Prima facie similarities in measures are thwarted in practice in the different systems wherein they are found. Confinement in a special institution for juvenile delinquents can occur as an ordinary punishment (as in Denmark), as a special juvenile punishment (as in the Netherlands, Italy or Germany), or as a purely educative measure (as in Belgium). A cautioning is a punishment in the Netherlands, an educative measure in Belgium and France and a special disciplinary measure in Germany. Community service is offered as an opportunity for diversion at the level of prosecution, or as an educational directive, a disciplinary measure or even as a condition for probation by the court in Germany. It can be part of the educational supervision conditions in Belgium, a diversionary measure or a probation condition in the Netherlands; it is a specific sanction within the juvenile penal justice in Italy and in England, where, in the latter, it can only be imposed from the age of 16 onwards. This chaotic situation illustrates how very different discourses can hide very similar practices and how similar discourses accompany different practices.

The most atypical 'juvenile punishment' is imposed in England and Wales, where parents themselves can be subjected to measures. They can be subject to a 'compensation order' or a 'bind-over', which implies a kind of supervision of their educative performance. It indicates that they are considered responsible for the offence of their child. Of course certain measures can be imposed on parents in other countries also, but then it happens as part of the 'protective jurisdiction' of 'children in danger'.

Conclusion: the ongoing struggle with the justice/welfare balance

All countries have tried to construct a kind of synthesis or compromise between two basic principles that are very hard to reconcile.

1. An offence demands a coercive and curbing approach. Penal law is attributed several functions: to restore, by retribution, the juridico-moral order that was disturbed by the offence; to keep possible offenders from committing a crime by deterrence; and even, if possible, to reform the offenders. Moreover, legal rules guarantee the legality of the intervention, the correctness of the trial, and the proportionality of the sanction.
2. A minor is not yet an adult. This implies that he is not yet capable of full responsibility and that he is still subject to socialising. The deterrence of the penal law is not functional for him. Moreover, it could cause negative effects on the socialising of the minor. The public reaction to an offence committed by a minor should, therefore, in the first place have an educative aim.

Both these ratios are fundamentally irreconcilable. A punishment refers to a fact in the past, the offence. The offence is the reason for the intervention, and the scale on which the intervention can be measured. This way the legality and the proportionality of the offence can be guaranteed. An educative measure, however, refers to an objective in the future, viz. an autonomous and conforming individual. The measure is no longer linked to a determinable offence, but to the needs of the person, which makes the use of the legal rules very hard. The link with the offence becomes vague, the proportionality cannot be measured anymore, the guarantees for the trial become misty.

The constructions most countries have tried out to reconcile both approaches are variations on the same 'mystifications du langage' (Van de Kerchove 1976–77).

In Belgium all punishments for minor delinquents have theoretically been abolished and all measures are called educative. In practice 'educative measures' are pronounced with a retributive undertone. The consequence is not a jurisdiction without punishments, but punishments without legal safeguards.

The so-called 'pedagogic penal law' that applies in the Netherlands, France, Italy or Germany remains ambiguous. Contrary to what is sometimes pretended, judicial punishment cannot be compared to punishment in an educative situation (for example in a family). The effectiveness of an educative punishment is connected to specific intrinsic and contextual conditions which are far from being realised in the (juvenile) court systems (Van Doosselaere 1988).

The more explicit division between the administrative welfare-approach and the judicial interventions, as they are worked out in Denmark and in Scotland, raises questions about the legal rules when the administrative agency can impose coercive measures, and it seems to lead to a higher use of the regular penal law for minor delinquents. England and Wales seem to use a more explicit penal regime for their youngsters with a more precise set of legal rules. But according to some criticisms this leads to exaggerated and ineffective punishments (Hudson 1987).

Generally speaking we must conclude that time and again the synthesis of penal law and educative principles has compounded the drawbacks of both systems. The legal guarantees are reduced and the educative quality is diminished.

In search of an alternative

These criticisms have, over the past decade, given rise to a variety of ideas for correction and adaptation. Various international organisations have laid down minimum rules and recommendations as to the legal guarantees to be assured for minors. The so-called Beijing Rules are considered a most important instrument to improve the intrinsic quality of jurisdiction towards juveniles all over the world. They provide indeed a series of clear statements about the minimum rules to be respected by all judicial interventions against juveniles (Doek 1991). Nevertheless, ambivalence persists. It is easy to state that the judicial reaction 'should be in proportion to both the offender and the offence' (Rule 5.1), but it is very difficult to combine both proportions on the field. How to 'allow appropriate scope for discretion at all stages of proceedings' (Rule 6.1.) and to assure at the same time 'the principles of fair and just trial' (Rule 14.1)? Actually, the proclamation of basic principles for the special jurisdiction for juveniles cannot avoid its basic problem, that is, the impossible combination, hidden by the 'mystification du language' mentioned above.

Other comments are pleading for a return to a more explicitly penal approach. Youth is more capable of making decisions and of bearing responsibility than has been assumed, it is said. As a consequence, young people should be treated as responsible individuals if they commit offences. In the United States, the growing concern about juvenile violence and legal problems, raised after several Supreme Court decisions, led several authors to propose the abolition of the juvenile court and to refer youthful offenders to the adults' court (Hirschi and Gottfredson 1991).

Return to penal justice is no solution at all (Walgrave 1985). The retributivist justifications of penal justice are based upon a naive classicist view of mankind and society and canalise revenge within the procedures of a constitutional state. This cannot be sufficient to govern a society. At least, instrumentalist arguments should be added to this.

Empirical research has clearly shown that the instrumentalist ambitions of penal law are not met.

Punitive prevention (or deterrence) is far less general than may be thought. It is effective only in certain conditions, for certain offences and certain types of offenders. Especially for juveniles, deterrence seems hardly to result in any effect (Schneider 1990). It would seem to be more the exception than the rule for an offender to be reformed by application of the conventional penalties of criminal law. On the contrary, in fact, various studies suggest that they have a marginalising and labelling effect (for example Lipton, Martinson and Wilkes 1975). The preservation of the victim's rights is certainly not central in the existing penal justice procedures. Other existing systems are far more effective in addressing the rights and needs of victims (Wright 1991). Therefore, many arguments in favour of the instrumentality of penal law would seem to be more cosmetic than based on established facts (Trepanier 1989).

Diversion has been proposed as a means of avoiding the labelling and other negative risks of the complete judicial procedure (Lemert 1971). Actually, diversion is an empty concept. It only indicates what is to be avoided, but not what is really done instead.

A lot of different types of intervention are presented to replace the judicial procedure: simple non-intervention, original or traditional types of treatment or assistance, victim/offender mediation, some kinds of community service. The procedure can be diverted at the police level or at the level of the public prosecutor, in co-operation with extra-judicial instances, or not. All these different forms of diversion are not better *per se*, just because they avoid the complete judicial procedure.

Very often they are problematic themselves, as they can be as stigmatising as the judgment by the court, including a manifest risk of net-widening and, especially, as they do not respect all legal safeguards that should be respected in a procedure against a person suspected of having committed an offence. The quality of diversion depends on the quality of the replacing model, not on the diversion mechanism itself.

Experiments with the so called 'alternative sanctions', sometimes as a form of diversion, illustrate the quest for new strategies in dealing with juvenile offenders.

The expression 'alternative sanctions' embraces a miscellany of practices, innovative rehabilitation programmes, novel educative and therapeutic programmes, pure compensation, community service and much more besides. All these programmes differ markedly in their objectives, basic philosophies, legal status and scope. The free experimenting has led to these so-called alternative sanctions being lumped together as a variegated collection with all the existing sanctions and measures, thus depriving them of their truly innovative aspect. It is time to abolish the catch-all term of 'alternative sanctions' and to indicate clearly what we are doing, certainly when the sanctions are formally included into the judicial system.

The catch-all term of alternative sanctions has been hiding one of the most promising developments in experimenting with new judicial intervention schemes, namely those with victim/offender mediation and community service. Almost all European countries do try out in one or another form a measure or a sanction that includes unpaid work for the benefits of the victim or of a social institution (Dunkel and Zermatten 1990). The success of these intervention schemes can be understood, because they fit into dominant tendencies in thinking about social reactions to crime and delinquency.

- The traditional rehabilitative measures were shown to be rather ineffective, so that new models were badly needed. The search was for sanctions that would fit more into the view on juveniles as able to bear responsibilities, and to compensate for the injuries done to the victim and society (Junger-Tas 1988).

- The new intervention schemes could contribute to avoiding the overburdening of the traditional system, by diverting non-relevant cases to extra-judicial agencies. On the other hand, this argument could also lead to a form of net-widening (Council of Europe 1993).
- The legal guarantees are often inaccurately respected in the traditional juvenile justice interventions, as they are more oriented to the person of the offender than to the offence itself. The possible reassessment of the offence as the reason of the sanction and as a measure for the gradation of the sanction in mediation and community service offers opportunities for a correct application of basic legal principles, such as legality, proportionality or due process.

These considerations and the growing confidence in the applicability of community service and victim/offender mediation on the field, have given rise to a tendency in thinking on judicial response to crime typified as restorative justice. According to that movement, the main objective of judicial intervention against an offence should not be to punish, not even to (re)educate, but to repair or to compensate for the harm caused by the offence (Barnett 1977).

The prospects of restorative justice for juveniles

Mediation and community service: two basic schemes of the same restorative justice

The origins of the concept restorative justice are to be found in the experiments with victim/offender mediation. One can understand that. The harm caused by the offence to the individual victim is visible and can (to some extent) be measured. The way of repairing or compensating for the harm can be negotiated. An agreement between the victim and the offender about the size and the kind of compensation or reparation can be observed. The implementation of the agreement can be monitored.

However, societal reaction to an offence cannot be restricted to reparation on its own, because it would reduce the official response to delinquency to a regulation according to civil law. Civil law is reactive, that is, active only after the lodging of a complaint. But a criminalised behaviour has been referred to penal law, because penal law is proactive, that is, has the option to prosecute on its own initiative. This referral proves the presence of other interests, besides the victim and the offender. In an offence, three parties are concerned: the victim, the offender and 'the community'. Society or the State sets itself up as the defender of the 'fundamental values, necessary to preserve social life', and, therefore, a system of penal law has been introduced. Even if no specific victims are complaining, society can intervene in order to preserve respect for these 'fundamental values' and for 'social life'.

If 'social order and legality', being the 'safeguards of the fundamental values' are harmed by crime the question of how can it be repaired is raised. Here is where community service comes to the fore. The community has been 'victimised' by the disruption of public order and by the threat to the public values, and it can demand a compensation for this by imposing a (compensatory) service to the community. From the one who caused a deterioration in community life, the community can demand an effort in favour of the community. The compensation will only have a symbolic aspect, but is not therefore less important (Messmer and Otto 1992).

Both mediation and community service are complementary parts of an ethico-juridical tendency identified as restorative justice. They have in common (1) a definition of crime as an injury to victims (concrete and societal); (2) the orientation towards restoration; (3) the active and direct implication of the offender in the restoration; and (4) the judicial framework, making possible the use of coercive power and of legal moderation as well.

Three models of judicial intervention

The appearance of a restorative approach to justice makes clear that we are confronted with three distinct models of reacting against crime: retributive, rehabilitative and restorative justice. Their essentials are presented in Table 9.2.

In practice, the differences are less clear-cut and more nuanced than the table might suggest. In conventional penal law, retribution is the primary means: the wilful inflicting of harm on an offender is an attempt to right the upset to the balance of the juridico-moral order. Recent doctrine also ascribes a resocialising function to penal law, although this is not demonstrated clearly by the empirical research. It is also presumed that the sanction affords a degree of satisfaction to the victim, which in itself would constitute a sort of compensation.

Table 9.2 Three basic models of reacting to juvenile crime

	Retributive	*Rehabilitative*	*Restorative*
Reference	Offence	Criminal person	Losses
Means	Inflicting a harm	Treating the person	Obligation to repair
Objectives	Juridico-moral balance	Conformism	Elimination of losses
Victim's position	Secondary	Secondary	Central
Criteria of Evaluation	Just desert	Conforming behaviour	Satisfaction of parties
Societal context	State of power	Welfare state	Responsible state

In penal law, the democratic state is at odds with itself: while claiming that it functions to preserve the citizens' rights and freedoms, it establishes a penal law system which restricts those very liberties. It reduces the state/citizen relations to one of simple duress in a power structure.

In rehabilitative justice, the emphasis is placed on treatment of the offending person: attempts are made, through personalised measures, to inhibit the offender from reoffending in the future. The treatment is not proposed, but imposed. Restrictions on liberty allied to the measure imposed also conceal a distasteful element of added hardship. This is not the intention, but an inevitable side-effect. To many victims, the rehabilitative reaction appears unfair: wrongdoers are not punished but helped, while they themselves have difficulty in securing recognition of their status as a victim and of being awarded compensation.

The rehabilitative approach is central to the welfare state, which operates for the well-being of its members, but only subject to disciplinary conditions of conformity.

The restorative justice paradigm places the emphasis on restitution of wrongs and losses – losses being understood as encompassing material damage, mental suffering and social injury alike. The victim may be an individual citizen or the community. The obligation to make good is restrictive for freedom, which may be acutely disagreeable. Unlike penal law, the added hardship is not an end as such, but a side-effect.

The obligation to make reparations also entails a confrontation, and may also entail a personal undertaking from the offender, which may 'teach him a lesson'. This educative effect is not the primary aim, however, but may be an added bonus. Mediation and community service are first and foremost a reactions to behaviour.

It is

> a reinforcement of the juridical position of minors according to the 'due process' model; less emphasis on protection and care, but more on the responsibility of the young; less attention to the personality of the offender and more to the victims of the offence; more emphasis on demanding compensation and reparation of the harm to the victim, be it the private person or the community. (Junger-Tas 1988, p.25)

The advantage of the restorative approach over the rehabilitative is clear: the reference to the losses again provides a more measurable yardstick than the 'needs of the individual' from which the legal guarantees can be deduced. Compared to the retributive approach, the restorative reaction is more constructive and less excluding. The type of state which makes it feasible is empowering and willing to negotiate. According to Braithwaite's theory, one could say that this is a communitarianist state, allowing the reintegrative shaming of the offender (Braithwaite 1989).

The growing confidence in the restorative approach

The idea that restorative justice could be a fully fledged alternative instead of being just a series of techniques to be inserted into the rehabilitative or the retributive models of judicial reacting to crime, is rather recent in modern jurisprudence.

Theoretical ethical and juridical reflection about restorative justice is developing. The principles guiding the restorative justice are explored and compared to those of the retributive or the rehabilitative approaches. The concept of restorative justice fits very well into the 'reintegrative shaming' theory, proposed by Braithwaite. According to Braithwaite, labelling can be the most powerful strategy to achieve low crime rates, in prevention as well as in social reaction against committed offences. The assumption, therefore, is that labelling leads to reintegrative shaming and not to stigmatisation and exclusion. 'Re-integrative shaming means that expressions of community disapproval...are followed by gestures of re-acceptance into the community of law-abiding citizens' (Braithwaite 1989). This happens in a 'communitarianist' society, that is, combining 'dense networks of individual interdependencies with strong cultural commitments to mutual obligation' (Braithwaite 1989).

The ethical bases of restorative justice are considered to be superior. Aiming at the solution of a conflict and at the reparation of the losses seems to be more constructive for social life than balancing an abstract juridico-moral order (Christie 1978). Instead of the ruling class norms like civic duty, conventional moralism or right to property, deeper social values like solidarity, peaceful social relations, social justice and equity come to the fore.

As the amount of empirical evidence is increasing, positive expectations are likewise developing. The willingness of victims to participate in mediation programmes, and their satisfaction after participation, are surprisingly high, taking into account the unconventional proposition they are confronted with and the novelty of the mediation technique itself (Umbreit and Coates 1992).

The scientific assessment of the effects on the offenders is extremely difficult, due to several methodological problems (Sechrest and Rosenblatt 1987). The reported results are not unambiguous, but no research shows a significant increase in recidivism (Messmer and Otto 1992). The differences in effects are probably due to the differences in the strategies of implementation. If measured, all programmes seem to result in a greater satisfaction and more feelings of equity than the traditional intervention schemes do.

Some programmes have examined the attitude of the public towards the restorative responses to crime. It is quite clear that the public is in general more willing to accept such an approach than most of the political and juridical authorities would like us to believe. If the restitutive opportunity is presented in a realistic way, the majority of the population responds in favour of that type of social reaction (Galaway 1984). The seriousness and the type of offence do not play the decisive role in that choice.

As things are for the moment, principles and theories, as well as the results of practical experiments and research, are still consistent with the maximalist hypothesis that restorative justice is a fully valid alternative to the retributive and the rehabilitative models of justice. Of course, a lot of problems persist. They can only be resolved through experimenting and research. The remaining questions can be divided into two major fields: (1) the juridical status of restorative justice and its basic schemes, mediation and community service; and (2) the practical limits of its applicability.

Exploring restorative justice as a fully fledged juridical approach

In search of a juridical status: restorative justice and democracy

At present, experiments in restorative orientation must take place within a retributive or rehabilitative justice system, which makes it hard to preserve the integrity of its legal concepts and status. Mediation and community service take place within or outside the system, at varying stages in the judicial process, with a wide variety of objectives and techniques. It is a miscellaneous profusion, an odd assortment of good intentions, opportunism and clear visions. It is an uncontrolled growth which may at times conflict with fundamental principles which govern the function of justice in a democratic state. Especially two qualities of a correct legal procedure are threatened: due process and proportionality.

Restorative justice is based on negotiation, which might jeopardise the course of a due process. It is essential that the rights of the parties concerned be preserved. Undue pressure on victims can conflict with his right not to engage in a mediation operation and could lead to a sort of secondary victimisation (Wright 1991).

Less formal procedures may also provoke less attention to legal rights of the offender, such as presumption of innocence, right to a defence, and right to a proportionate sanction (Feest 1993). In mediation, young offenders, for example, might through ignorance or lack of an advocate be pressured into accepting a mediation outcome which has weightier consequences for them than if they had submitted to the due process of ordinary law. Unequal power relations and/or social prestige of the victim and the socially vulnerable young offender may also have similar results. That is why principles of a due process must be respected very carefully.

One could accept that victim/offender mediation could be used as a diversion strategy. The opportunity for a victim to obtain satisfaction without setting the entire penal machinery in motion reduces his need to have recourse to the penal system; therefore, the prosecutor may make successful mediation a condition for non-prosecution, or the court may make compensation a condition of probation. As we have seen in the first part of this chapter, this is fairly current practice in many European countries. For the preservation of the rights of the parties we just mentioned, it remains important that mediation be carried out under (possibly indirect) judicial supervision.

As regards community service the position is different. Community service must expressly be seen as a sanction. There is no question here of settlement of loss by negotiated agreement. The public prosecutor, as the representative of the community, claims a compensation for the injury to social life through community service. Therefore, community service expressly embodies a restriction on liberty imposed as a result of crime. The degree of guilt for the offence and the extent of the compensation, that is, the extent of community service, cannot be fixed by the prosecutor himself. In Western democratic legal systems, this can be done only by the court. The link between the offence and the action taken in respect of it is less direct than in mediation. Defining that link becomes more difficult and delicate, therefore. Consequently, judgement on it must be reserved until the procedure has run its full course.

In the European practices we described previously, this is certainly not always the case. Community service is imposed (or 'proposed') by the court, the prosecuting authority, and even, on occasion, by the police. This 'experimental flux' poses a problem with respect to the principle of due process, certainly if it were to be inserted into legal dispositions as a regular model of intervention.

Defining the link between the offence and the sanction poses the issue of proportionality. It is one of the most difficult problems for restorative justice.

Proportionality means that the intensity of the sanction (expressed in the degree and duration of the restriction on liberty), should be in proportion to the seriousness of the crime to be sanctioned. In retributive justice, the punishment should be a just desert (Von Hirsch 1976). In principle, proportionality has been fixed in our penal legislation, based on tradition and on socio-juridical negotiations between conflicting interests in society. Proportionality in penal law is not an objective quality, but the result of a socio-legal convention.

The idea of proportionality has been abandoned in most juvenile justice systems, as its reference was not to the offence any more, but to the offender. But even here, proportionality is being restored as a point of interest, thanks to international conventions like the Bejing Rules.

Proportionality in restorative justice would refer neither to seriousness of the offence, nor to the person of the offender, but to the amount of harm caused by the offence. How do we define that?

In victim/offender mediation the realisation of proportionality is in the hands of the mediating parties. Not only does material damage have to be taken into account, but also, and often much more so, the psychosocial damage, which is very difficult to measure and to gauge in terms of compensation. Nevertheless, most mediations end in an agreement, so that we can theoretically assume that victim and offender have reached their common view of a sort of proportionality.

It becomes more difficult to measure the harm to social life, for which community service would be the compensation. What kind of harm do we have to take into account? For the moment, the definition of 'public losses' is still vague. Van Ness points to 'loss of public safety, damage to community values and the disruption caused by crime' (Van Ness 1990). Sometimes these are very direct and concrete, if public goods have been stolen or vandalised. Very often, public losses are indirect. Crime can be a shocking attack on public values and norms. It affects solidarity and mutual respect, both necessary for harmonious community life. It causes feelings of insecurity, worsening the quality of life. Delinquency necessitates the existence of very expensive systems of prevention and social reaction. Anyway, it cannot be denied that collectivity suffers damage from the delinquency and the offence.

How can this damage be measured? We lack reliable measurements to express the amount of public harm in terms that could be linked to an amount of compensation through a service to community. There is no tradition of it and public socio-juridical negotiations have not taken place yet. That is why practice is so unequal (Walgrave and Geudens 1994). However, this disproportionality is not linked to the theoretical concept of restorative justice, but to the immaturity of existing practice all over the world. One can assume that the increase in experience, and in communication among the practices and among juridical and criminological academicians, will yield some general indicators for measuring proportionality in community service in future.

One might wonder whether the restorative order of the offence, according to the losses to social life, will finally deviate so much from the existing retributive order, according to the perceived seriousness of the offence. After all, by what criterion is seriousness guaged now?

In search of the limits to restorative justice: just a technique or a fully valid alternative?

The most important question for further experimenting and research is, of course, the one about the limits of the restorative approach. Is restorative approach just a technique, to be inserted as a complement into existing retributive or rehabilitative systems, or can it develop as a fully valid alternative of its own, for both systems? Theoretically, we can think of four different types of limitations.

THE SERIOUSNESS OF THE OFFENCE

In practice, restorative techniques have been mostly applied to less serious offences and offenders. We accept that a simple victim/offender mediation cannot be sufficient as a single societal answer to serious offences. The seriousness of the offence includes the gravity of the disturbance to social life, so that the community as victim can demand compensation also. But it is difficult to find a good reason to exclude serious offenders from community service.

- The idea that serious offenders have to undergo a really punitive experience goes back to the purely retributive interpretation of penal justice. Revenge, even when from within a legal framework, is not a sufficient basis for a civilised social reaction. It should at least be complemented by more social and efficiency-related considerations.
- The statement that 'the public' would not accept the imposition of community service on serious offenders relies on a stereotype. The existing research, briefly mentioned above, shows that the public does not react in as punitive a way as is sometimes suggested. Even most of the direct victims of the offences prefer a restorative response to a purely punitive one.
- The assumption that serious offenders cannot be influenced positively by community service rests upon a naive etiological assumption that is not confirmed by empirical research. The existing data suggest that serious offenders are capable of fulfilling a community

service order and of feeling the benefits of it, without an increase in the risk of recidivism (De Martelaere and Peeters 1985).

THE CO-OPERATION OF THE CONCERNED

The limit to restorative justice could be related to the willingness of those concerned to co-operate.

If the victim refuses to co-operate in a mediation programme, mediation is impossible. However, the refusal of the victim is not a stable nor a purely objective element. It is a response to a proposal to mediate. In many cases, the way in which that proposal has been made is decisive for its acceptance or not (Umbreit 1988). But if the victim refuses, there is still community service.

What if the offender refuses the mediation and community service? Obviously, the refusal or the acceptance are relative here, as they are at least partly depending on the way mediation or community service are propsed and controlled. But even in case of a refusal to cooperate in community service, we cannot totally exclude that such a service would be imposed (possibly in a residential setting).

SECURITY REASONS

Security reasons are often quoted as the reasons for restricting the implementation of restorative techniques, which have to be carried out in the community. In some cases, the risks of serious recidivism would be too high.

Nor is imprisonment absolutely safe either. A great diversity of models and regimes of imprisonment exist. Many prisoners have periods of unsupervised contacts with society. The fact itself that relatively few incidents occur proves that for the moment many offenders who are locked up could perfectly well undertake reparation or community service within the freedom of society, without serious security risks.

Detention itself does not exclude restorative objectives and several authors have proposed maintaining incarceration until a given goal of reparation or compensation has been achieved (Spencer 1975 quoted in Weitekamp 1992).

THE NEED FOR REHABILITATION

The need for rehabilitation is a priority that could hamper the introduction of a fully restorative justice approach. Rehabilitation of the offender is an objective of high moral standing and thus a worthy objective. But it does not limit the use of restoration.

In many cases, restorative techniques are used in a rehabilitative way. Mediation or community service is not used with a view to repair or compensate for the losses, but in order to (re)educate the offender. There are two kinds of objections to such a practice. (1) The victims' right to compensation is not recognised as such, and they serve only as 'educative demonstrative factors' in the treatment of the offenders. (2) Rehabilitative interventions are oriented towards the personality of the offender, which makes it more difficult to safeguard legal guarantees, such as the legality of the intervention, or the proportionality of the sanction.

But a restorative intervention within the justice system does not exclude a rehabilitative offer outside the justice process. One can imagine that the judicial obligation to restore could run parallel to the offer of help by a welfare agency. The restorative ethics and techniques are not contradictory to the rehabilitative ones.

Finally, as the evidence demonstrates, the rehabilitative effects of the restorative approaches are not less than those of the approaches aimed explicitly at rehabilitation. Within the limits of proportional community service, the kind of service to be accomplished can be chosen with educative criteria in mind (Bazemore and Maloney 1994). The very fact of being obliged to make good the harm which has been done often seems to have a rehabilitative effect that goes beyond the traditional models of treatment. But, let there be no misunderstanding: this is not the prior objective of restorative justice. It is only a positive side-effect.

Conclusion

In Europe, as in the USA, discussions about the juvenile justice systems are, as ever, ongoing. They have repeatedly centred on finding a satisfying balance between welfare concerns and the judicial coercive approach. Every country has botched together its own system, sustained by inventive 'mystifications du language' (Van de Kerchove 1976–77), but the doctoring and arguing have always continued. At present, the discussion seems to have reached an impasse. The pure, one-sided welfare approach has been a humane, but naive dream. For minor offences, it is very often a kind of overacting, risking stigmatisation. For some kinds of urban juvenile crime, it seems ineffective and even sometimes ridiculous.

These observations have led to a strong tendency in the USA towards the abolition of the juvenile justice system and for a return to the traditional penal settlement of juvenile crime. In Europe too, many countries have recently added some punitive elements in their legislation, or they are in process of doing so.

But re-penalising of juvenile offending is simply a return to the negative cruelty of a retributive system of revenge. The negative characteristics of penal law, which were the reasons for our legislators withdrawing juveniles from it at the beginning of the century, still exist. Its implementation is not so much a victory of justice, as is sometimes triumphantly asserted. It is in the first place a defeat for society: offending means that society has failed to offer some people enough of the gratifications that motivate conformity; penal sanctions are needed because society has been unable to offer the victim and the offender a more constructive way of resolving their conflict. As Radbruch says: 'The best reform of penal law consists of its replacement, not by a better penal law, but by something better' (Tulkens 1993). Something better has to be looked for in the restorative direction. It is a way out of the unfruitful welfare/justice dilemma and a means to escape the panicky repressive reactions in the USA.

Of course, restorative justice will also have its limits, but they are not yet known. For the moment, the restorative justice model is a paradigm, orienting reflection and experimenting on the judicial response to crime and delinquency. The experiments have mostly been overcautious, restricted too much to cases with small risks to the community (but taking the risk of net widening) and they had to be carried out within a rehabilitative or retributive context. But as they are developing, the possibilities of the restorative justice approach are augmenting and the need to appeal to the traditional systems is decreasing. We do not know yet just where these developments are going to lead us.

The restorative justice model will never be the only one in reacting against delinquency but it could eventually become dominant.

The limitations of the retributive model have not hampered its dominance in the traditional approach of crime. Society accepts that the negativity and the cruelty of retribution cannot be applied to everyone and it, therefore, creates separate judicial systems for juveniles and for the insane. Moreover, a huge section of recorded offenders is deliberately not prosecuted. Finally, the negative effects on the offenders and the absence of positive effects for the victims (to put it mildly) are generally accepted, and these socio-ethical limitations are not considered as reasons for abolishing the retributive system.

The rehabilitative model is dominant in the judicial approach to juveniles, but this system is limited by the demands for correct legal safeguards (which are often neglected), by the need for co-operation by the 'rehabilitated' juvenile (which is often hidden behind the illusions of 'coercive assistance' and 'educative penal interventions'), and for security reasons.

The idea that restorative justice as the dominant approach could replace the retributive and the rehabilitative models is not just an academic hypothesis. It is also a socio-ethical objective. Giving priority to reparation rather than to retribution calls for a change in social ethics and a different ideology in society. It is based on a belief in a communitarian society that draws its strength not from fear but from the high social ethics by which it is governed; that avoids, as far as possible, excluding its deviant members, but instead tries instead to reintegrate them by gestures of reintegrative shaming.

Is this utopianism? Yes, but we need a utopia to motivate us and provide guidance for our actions in society. There is nothing more practical than a good utopia.

References

Barnett, R. (1977) Restitution: a new paradigm of criminal justice. In R. Barnett and J. Hagel (eds) *Assessing the Criminal*. Cambridge: Ballinger.

Basta, J. and Davidson, W. (1988) Treatment of juvenile offenders: study outcomes since 1980. *Behavioral Sciences and the Law 6*, 355–384.

Bazemore, G. and Maloney, D. (1994) Rehabilitating community service. Toward restorative service sanctions in a balanced justice system. *Federal Probation*, March, 24–35.

Braithwaite, J. (1989) *Crime, Shame and Reintegration*. Cambridge: Cambridge University Press.

Christie, N. (1978) Conflicts as property. *British Journal of Criminology 17*, 1–15.

Council of Europe (ed.) (1993) Social Strategies and the Criminal Justice System. Proceedings of the 19th Criminological Research Conference, November 1990. Strasbourg: Council of Europe.

De Martelaere, G. and Peeters, J. (1985) Een experiment van alternatieve sancties aan de jeugdrechtbank te Mechelen. *Panopticon 1*, 34–54.

Doek, J. (1991) The future of the juvenile court. In J. Junger-Tas, L. Boendermaker and P. van der Laan (eds) *The Future of the Juvenile Justice System*. Leuven: Acco.

Dünkel, F. and Meyer, K. (eds) (1985/86) *Jugendstrafe und Jugendstrafvollzug. Stationäre Massnahmen des Jugendkriminalrechstpflege im internationalen Vergleich*. 2 vols. Freiburg: Kriminologische Forschungsberichte aus dem Max-Planck-Institut.

Dünkel, F. and Zermatten J. (eds) (1990) *Nouvelles tendances dans le droit pénal des mineurs. Médiation, travail au profit de la communauté et traitement intermédiaire*. Freiburg, Kriminologische Forschungsberichte aus dem Max-Planck-Institut.

Feest, J. (1993) Courses of action designed to avoid entry in the criminal justice process or to interrupt the process. In Council of Europe (ed.) (1993).

Feld, B. (1993) Criminalizing the American Juvenile Court. In M. Tonry (ed.) *Crime and Justice: A Review of Research*. Vol. 17. Chicago: University of Chicago Press.

Galaway, B. (1984) A survey of public acceptance of restitution as an alternative to imprisonment for property offenders. *Australian and New Zealand Journal of Criminology* 2, 108–117.

Galaway, B. and Hudson, J. (1990) Towards restorative justice. In B. Galaway and J. Hudson (eds) *Criminal Justice, Restitution and Reconciliation*. Monsey: Willow Tree Press.

Heinz, J. (1984) Diversion und Schlichtung in der Bundesrepublik Deutschland. *Zeitschrift für die gesamte Strafrechtswissenschaft 6*, 455–484.

Hirschi, T. and Gottfredson, M. (1991) Rethinking the juvenile justice system. In T. Booth (ed.) *Juvenile Justice in the New Europe*. Sheffield: Social Services Monographs.

Hudson, B. (1987) *Justice Through Punishment*. London: MacMillan.

Institut de Sciences pénales et de Criminologie (ed.) (1992) *Droit Pénal Européen des mineurs*. Aix en Provence: Presses Universitaires d'Aix-Marseille.

Junger-Tas, J. (1988) Veranderingen in het gezin en reacties op delinquent gedrag. *Justitiële verkenningen 8*, 7–30.

Lemert, E. (1971) Instead of court. Maryland, National Institute of Mental Health, Crime and Delinquency Issues.

Lipton, D., Martinson, R. and Wilkes, J. (1975) *The Effectiveness of Corrections Treatment: A Survey of Treatment Evaluation Studies*. New York: Praeger.

Marshall, T. (1992) Restorative justice on trial in Britain. In H. Messmer and H. Otto (eds) *Restorative Justice on Trial*. Dordrecht/Boston: Kluwer Academic Publishers.

Mehlbye, J. and Walgrave, L. (eds) (1995) *Confronting Youth in Europe*. Copenhagen: AKF.

Messmer, H. and Otto, H.U. (eds) (1992) *Restorative Justice on Trial*. Dordrecht/Boston: Kluwer Academic Publishers.

Schafer, S. (1977) *Victimology. The Victim and his Criminal*. Reston: Prentice Hall.

Schneider, A. (1990) *Deterrence and Juvenile Crime*. New York: Springer.

Sechrest, J. and Rosenblatt, A. (1987) Research methods. In H. Quay (ed.) *Handbook of Juvenile Delinquency*. New York: Wiley.

Steinert, H. (1988) Kriminalität als Konflikt. *Kriminalsoziologische Bibliografie. Spezialheft 58/59*, 11–20.

Trepanier, J. (1989) Principes et objectifs guidant le choix des mesures prises en vertu de la loi sur les jeunes contrevenants. *Revue du Barreau 4*, 559–605.

Tulkens, F. (1993) Les transformations du droit pénal aux Etats-Unis. Pour un autre modèle de justice. In *Nouveaux itinéraires en droit. Hommage a Francis Rigaux*. Bruxelles: Bruylant.

Umbreit, M. (1988) Mediation of victim offender conflict. *Journal of Dispute and Resolution* 2, 85–105.

Umbreit, M. and Coates, R. (1992) *Victim Offender Mediation: An Analysis of Programs in Four States of the U.S.* Minneapolis: Minnesota Citizens Council on Crime and Justice.

United Nations Standard Minimum Rules for the Administration of Juvenile Justice (Beijing Rules, 1985).

United Nations Standard Minimum Rules for Juveniles Deprived of their Liberty (1990).

Van de Kerchove, M. (1976–77) Des mesures repressives aux mesures de sureté et de protection. Réflexions sur le pouvoir mystificateur du langage. *Revue de Droit Pénal et de Criminologie* 4, 245–279.

Van der Laan, P. (1991) *Experimenteren met Alternatieve Sancties Voor Minderjarigen*. Arnhem/Den Haag: Gouda Quint/WODC.

Van Doosselaere, D. (1988) Du stimulus aversif à la cognition sociale. L'efficacité de la sanction selon un modèle de psychologie experimentale. *Déviance et Société* 3, 269–287.

Van Hees, J. (1991) Diversion in the Netherlands: bureau Halt. In J. Junger-Tas, L. Boendermaker en P. van der Laan (eds) *The Future of the Juvenile Justice System*. Leuven: Acco.

Van Ness, D. (1990) Restorative justice. In B. Galaway and J. Hudson (eds) *Criminal Justice, Restitution and Reconciliation*. Monsey: Willow Tree Press.

Von Hirsch, A. (1976) *Doing Justice: The Choice of Punishments. Report of the Committee for the Study of Incarceration*. New York: Hill and Wang.

Walgrave, L. (1985) La repénalisation de la delinquance juvénile: une fuite en avant. *Revue de Droit Pénal et de Criminologie 7*, 603–623.

Walgrave, L. (1994) Beyond rehabilitation. In search of a constructive alternative in the judicial response to juvenile crime. *European Journal on Criminal Policy and Research* 2, 57–75.

Walgrave, L. (1995) Restorative justice for juveniles. Just a technique or a fully fledged alternative? *The Howard Journal of Criminal Justice 3*, 228–249.

Walgrave, L. and Geudens, H. (1994) Community service as a sanction of restorative justice. Paper presented at Meeting of the American Society of Criminology.

Weitekamp, E. (1992) Can restitution serve as a reasonable alternative to imprisonment? In H. Messmer and H. Otto (eds) *Restorative Justice on Trial*. Dordrecht/Boston: Kluwer Academic Publishers.

Wright, M. (1989) What the public wants. In M. Wright and B. Galaway (eds) *Mediation in Criminal Justice: Victims, Offenders and Community*. London: Sage.

Wright, M. (1991) *Justice for Victims and Offenders: A Restorative Approach to Crime*. Milton Keynes: Open University Press.

Wright, M. (1992) Victim–offender mediation as a step towards a restorative justice. In H. Messmer and H. Otto (eds) *Restorative Justice on Trial*. Dordrecht/Boston: Kluwer Academic Publishers.

The Contributors

Stewart Asquith	is St Kentigern Professor for the Study of the Child, Centre for the Study of the Child and Society, University of Glasgow.
Francis Bailleau	is Researcher, Centre National De Recherche Scientifique, Paris.
Jon Bright	is Director of Field Operations, Crime Concern.
James Garbarino	is Director, Family Life Development Center, and Professor of Human Development and Family Studies, Cornell University.
John Graham	is a member of the Research and Planning Unit, Home Office, London.
Kathleen Kostelny	is Senior Research Associate, Erikson Institute for Advanced Study in Child Development, Chicago.
Paul Littlewood	is Lecturer, Department of Sociology, University of Glasgow.
Derick McClintock	Late Professor of Criminology, University of Edinburgh.
Janice McGhee	is Researcher in the Department of Social Work, University of Edinburgh.
Alex Robertson	is Reader, Department of Social Policy, University of Edinburgh.
Elaine Samuel	is Researcher, Centre for Social Welfare Research, University of Edinburgh.
Kay Tisdall	is Lecturer, Centre for the Study of the Child and Society, University of Glasgow.
Lorraine Waterhouse	is Professor, Department of Social Work, Edinburgh University.
Lode Walgrave	is Professor of Juvenile Criminology at the Katholieke Universiteit, Leuven.
Bill Whyte	is Senior Lecturer in the Department of Social Work, Edinburgh University.